PEARLS OF A PATRIARCH;
and
Psychotherapeutic Anecdotes

Moshe Polter, MALPC

David Harp Publishers

Publisher is David Harp Publishers

ISBN-13: 978-0615985824
ISBN-10: 0615985823

Table of Contents

FOREWORD

"Schneur," he said, as he handed me this rubber-banded pile of papers, while lying deathly ill, nearing his end, in early January, 2005. "Take this," he continued as his cadence lowered to nearly inaudible, "and do with it what you did with The Shevatim. You've done well with that, and made me proud." He took a deep laborious breath. "Make sure to disseminate this, because armed with the knowledge and advice contained in this book, the world will be a better one."

I took the tattered ream from his pale fragile hands, as tears streamed down my face, knowing full well that my father of 34 years was nearing expiration. We hugged. I kissed him on his forehead. And through his pain and tears, he smiled at me, as he squeezed my hand in affirmation and approbation.

My father was born in 1938 in Antwerp, Belgium, the third of six children – at the time though the baby. As a child of only four years of age, he was forced to flee "by foot" Nazi-occupied Belgium because the Wehrmacht began their assault on Belgian Jewry without mercy and with unrelenting and unabashed menace and marauding. His family was lucky to have been from the very last ones to be granted asylum in neutral Switzerland, and he lived out the war years there. In about 1952, the family emigrated to Toronto, Ontario. In his early 20s, he arrived in Detroit, where he met a young Kayla Tennenbaum, and they married in 1961.

Dad was a fairly strict disciplinarian and was quite demanding of myself and my eight siblings. But one thing about Dad was this: He always practiced what he preached. *He lived this Book's morals and principles!* He wasn't one for laziness or excuses, and always aspired to bigger and better, and expected no less from us. A "C" was okay, but only if the effort was an "A". And *always respect your elders (especially mom)*, was his mantra. Violation of this mantra, was grounds for "capital", not corporal, punishment. Suffice it to say, he was real old-school, but with a unique sense of fairness, objectivity, humility and dignity.

The following story, one of many, epitomizes and personifies Dad, and demonstrates his overall unique classiness and *Mentchlichkeit* (No real equivalence in the English language exists for that term).

My father taught 4th grade at the Beth Jacob School for Girls in Detroit, for 33 years. Thirty years ago (1984), the school was in great financial distress, and was unable to pay its teachers. Realizing the crisis in their own households, as a result of unpaid wages, the teachers decided to strike. My father was extremely principled and found it difficult reconciling joining the strike; he just didn't believe it was the right thing at the time, and didn't believe it served any beneficial interest except to vent, which, in and of itself, is self-serving and counterproductive. On the other hand, due to practicality and comradery concerns, and not wishing to cross the picket line, he decided to join the strikers, though with a heavy heart.

One teacher, an elderly and scholarly fellow, and one who was truly *old* old school, did in fact cross the picket line and kept on teaching.

After about a week of striking, enough money was collected to at least partially pay the teachers. During the school meeting called to pay the teachers and get them back in the classrooms, my father spoke up and said: "In my opinion, Rabbi X should be paid first out of the monies we've secured. After all, he remained in the classroom throughout." You could well imagine the reception that statement received from the other teachers. Funds were thus distributed accordingly to all the striking teachers, and Rabbi X was left with nothing.

After getting paid, my father endorsed his own check, marched down to Rabbi X's classroom and handed it to the rabbi.

Although I'm certain you are fairly impressed with this story and the dignity and humility and class it portrays, there's an even better epilogue.

EPILOGUE: None of us, including mom, knew of this story until it was recounted twenty-two years later by Rabbi T.H. Kleinberg, one of the striking teachers (the only one who witnessed the entire incident), at Dad's *Shiva*.

Pop and I always shared an affinity for reading, researching and writing on a whole host of topics. We were both very studious and had a penchant for philosophy, philology, theology, esotericism and abstract thinking. We were both the "perpetual student".

Previously, Dad published several books (see "About the Author" section below) for which he won many accolades.

Now at the age of 45, I have authored four books – one of these co-authored with my late father. Another captures the splendor and nostalgia of the sport of Baseball, and the Village of Cooperstown, New York, the birth place and Mecca of the Sport. More recently though, and a book that's been in the works for more than seven years, and which I consider my true Magnum Opus: *God is Great; Setting the Record Straight*, David Harp Publishers, 2014, hit the bookshelves only months ago, and is one in which mine and Dad's passions meet.

I was therefore entrusted with the duty and honor of completing this work. It is in fact a work worthy of my time and painstaking diligence, but mostly it was his dying wish, one I pledged to complete.

And so now, on Dad's 10th Yahrtzeit (death anniversary) – a milestone in Jewish lore – I am proud to present you with this brilliant treasure.

Initially, Dad would come up with these short proverbs, pen them and mail them once per week to his clients, friends and colleagues – He referred to this compilation as *Think About It*. In compiling these and turning this into a book, I thought a more appropriate title was the one I've chosen, because these are indeed **Pearls** *of a "true"* **Patriarch**, and is a legacy by which he will be remembered. Of course it doesn't hurt that the acronym spells POPA (Father).

Dad was the consummate Patriarch. His Patriarchal status and stamina could be felt when we'd gather around a magnificently bedecked Passover Seder table – an evening that was so momentous for myself and my siblings, an evening that was so opulent and regal that we will not soon forget the grand presence and panache of father and mother as they sat on the dais flanked by children, grandchildren, other extended family, and a bevy of guests, along the nearly 15-foot table that protruded from the dais in T-like fashion.

Dad's patriarchal nature was further apparent when we'd all stand around the console especially constructed for all the flickering flames that emanated from the eight proud Menorahs that decorated the cozy home during those frigid Hanukkah nights, while listening intently as Dad mellifluously recited the blessings, as sparkling snowflakes fell just beyond the window.

How emotionally charging it was as dusk broke on the holiest day of the Jewish calendar. We were all clothed in our finest attire, and Dad was cloaked in his special bright white Yom Kippur garments. As he placed both hands on each of our heads and murmured several verses, he'd bless each of us carefully and tearfully, subsequent to which he'd kiss each forehead. Some of the older siblings would imagine *this must be what the Father of all fathers is doing just about now as His children are bound for the Day of Judgment.*

Indeed, the consummate Patriarch! And one who would march to his own beat, but who served as a true role model, and who died in class as he lived.

I am now proud to bring to you this tattered tear-drenched ream, handed to me by my Patriarch almost ten-years-ago to this day; now so beautifully adorned and decorated as is deserving of such a lifetime effort – Dad's third and final book.

It is my hope and prayer that you enjoy reading and re-reading and internalizing the contents hereof as much as I have enjoyed bringing it to you.

Rabbi Stephen Schneur Polter, JD, MBA

ABOUT THE AUTHOR

This book contains 283 wonderful anecdotes and expressions on life, all from the perspective of its author, Rabbi Dr. Moshe Polter, OBM, who composed and compiled these over a career that spanned more than four decades.

Rabbi Polter taught 4th grade Hebrew school in Detroit for 33 years. He also served as principal of a private elementary school, and was a licensed psychotherapist. He was a member of the American Counseling Association, Michigan Counseling Association, a diplomat of the American Psychotherapy Association, and was a Certified Addictions Counselor.

Rabbi Polter authored *The Shevatim* (The Tribes), Targum Press - Feldheim, 2004. He also co-authored two other works with renown psychotherapist, Dr. Morris Mandel: *More Wooing, Less Suing*, 2000; and *Verbal Vitamins for a Healthier Life*, 1998. Finally, Rabbi Polter also co-authored another book, with his son Schneur, *0 to 5760 in 60 Minutes*, a panoramic view of Jewish history, Spirit Press, 2006.

Besides the unique, new and novel thoughts and ideas contained herein, what is truly unique about this book over other similar ones, is the alphabetized index at the back, a phenomenal tool to guide you through life's trials and tribulations, enabling the reader to quickly tap in to a motivational thought to cheer him up in a down moment, or when life has thrown a curve ball of various shapes, sizes and trajectory.

You will as well no doubt find the Appendix to this book, a collection of essays with a similar theme as the Book's main thrust, highly engaging and enjoyable.

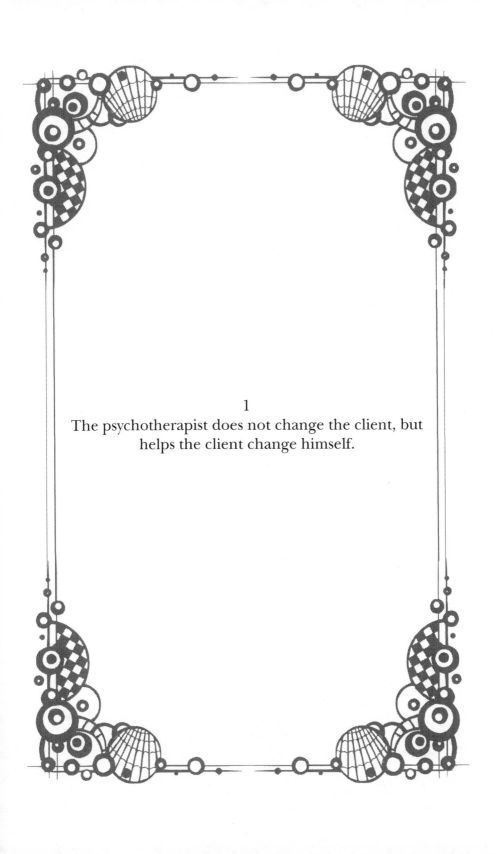

1
The psychotherapist does not change the client, but
helps the client change himself.

2

If you complain *less*, you will have *less*
to complain *about*.

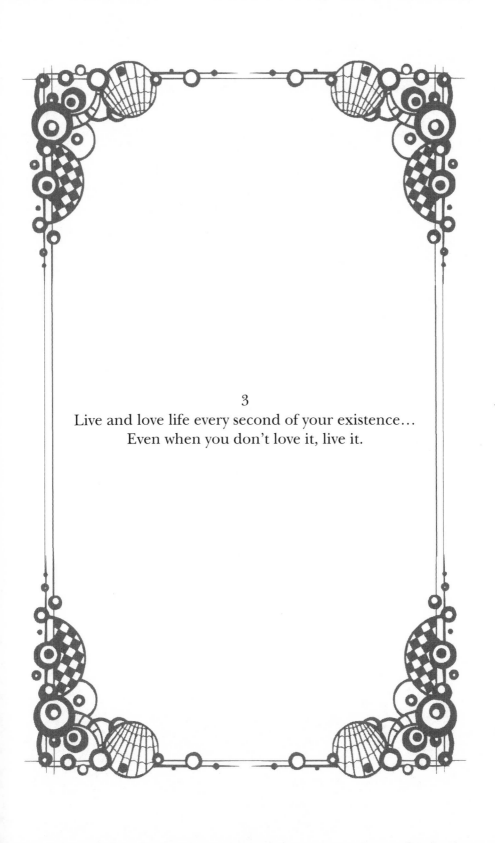

3
Live and love life every second of your existence…
Even when you don't love it, live it.

4

Do not "strain" but rather "train", and expand the
horizons of the brain.

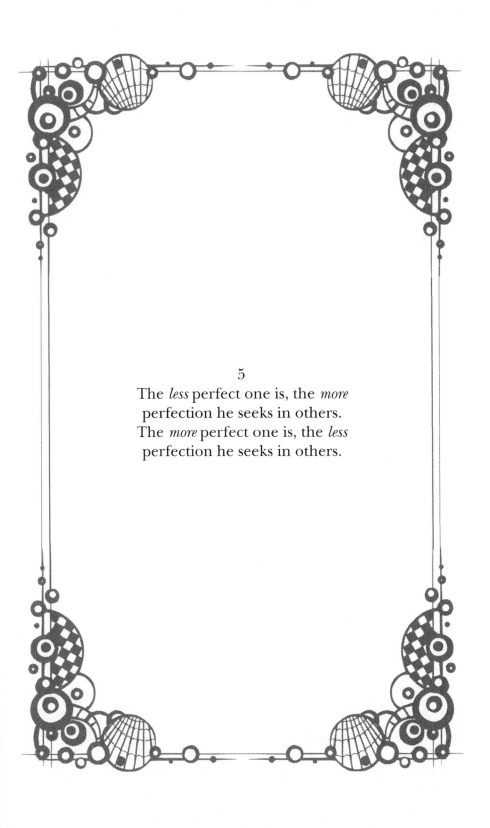

5

The *less* perfect one is, the *more*
perfection he seeks in others.
The *more* perfect one is, the *less*
perfection he seeks in others.

6

All the $$$ in the world spent on acquiring book knowledge will not buy an ounce of common ¢¢¢.

7

A cloudy sun is better than no sun at all.

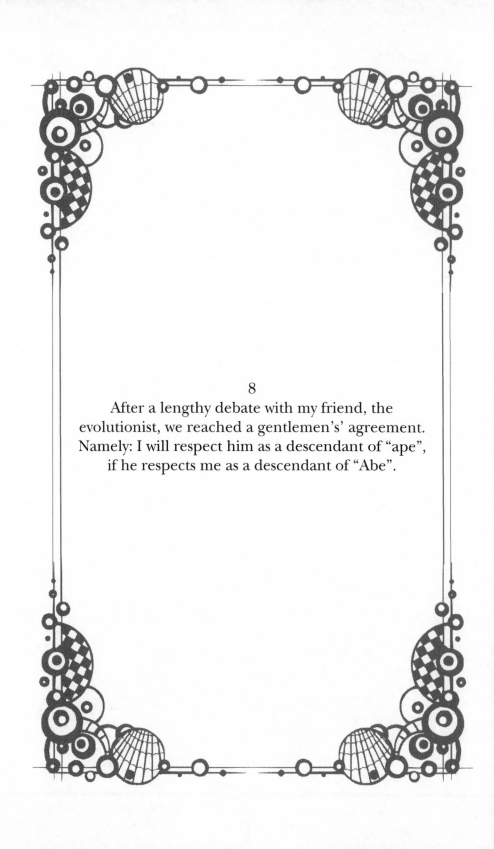

8

After a lengthy debate with my friend, the
evolutionist, we reached a gentlemen's' agreement.
Namely: I will respect him as a descendant of "ape",
if he respects me as a descendant of "Abe".

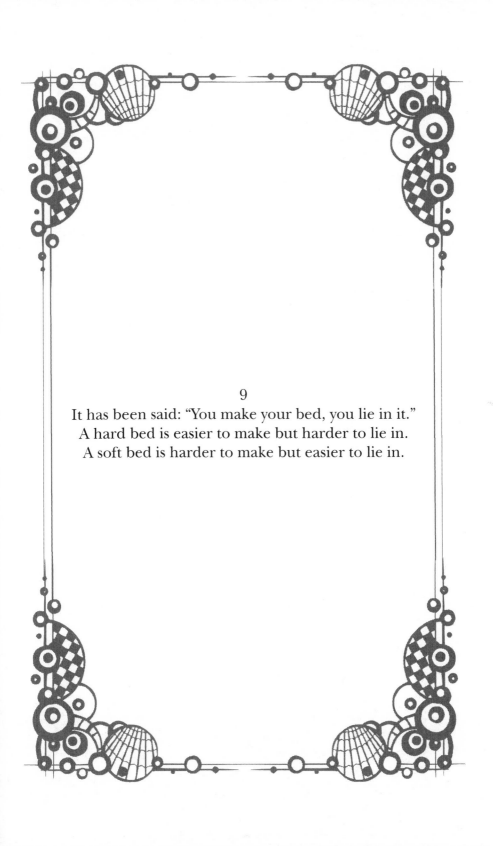

9

It has been said: "You make your bed, you lie in it."
A hard bed is easier to make but harder to lie in.
A soft bed is harder to make but easier to lie in.

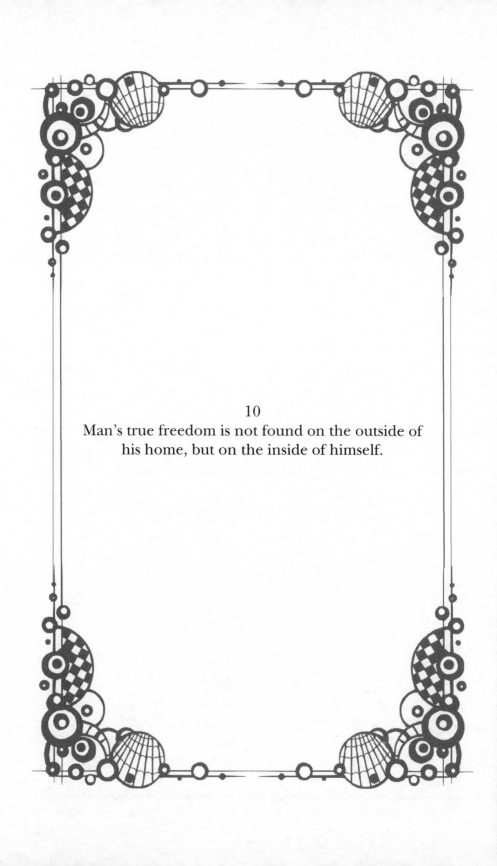

10

Man's true freedom is not found on the outside of his home, but on the inside of himself.

11
Time could be everything.
Time could be nothing.
It all depends on how it is utilized.

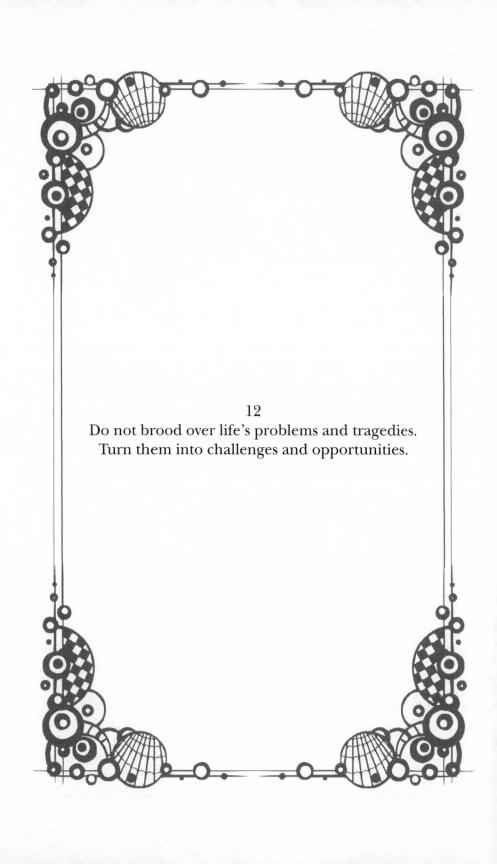

12
Do not brood over life's problems and tragedies.
Turn them into challenges and opportunities.

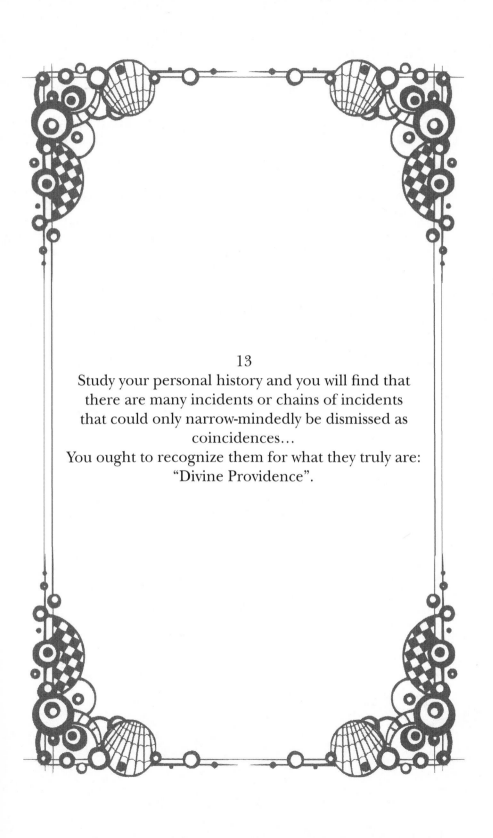

13
Study your personal history and you will find that
there are many incidents or chains of incidents
that could only narrow-mindedly be dismissed as
coincidences...
You ought to recognize them for what they truly are:
"Divine Providence".

14
Who said,
"Time is money"?
I say:
Time cannot be traded for any goods in
the world, including money.

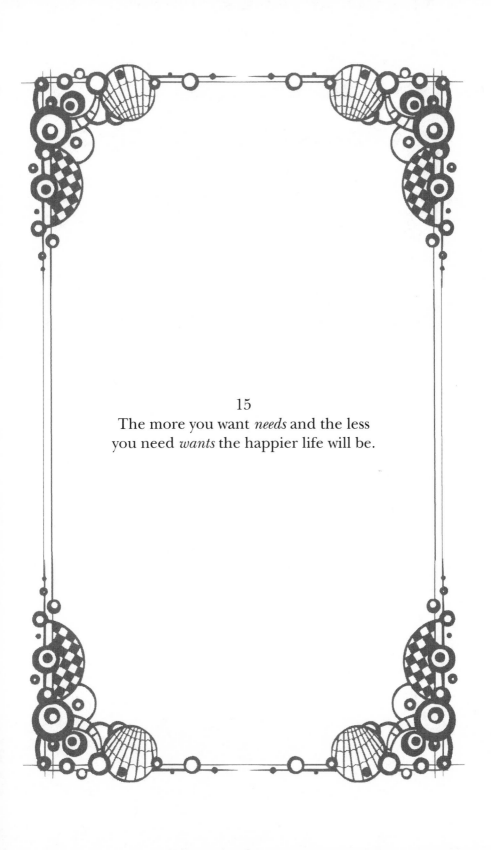

15
The more you want *needs* and the less
you need *wants* the happier life will be.

16
1. Strive for what you can.
2. Accept what you can't.
3. Appreciate what you have.

17
Doing enough of *nothing* will develop
into a full-time career of *doing nothing*.

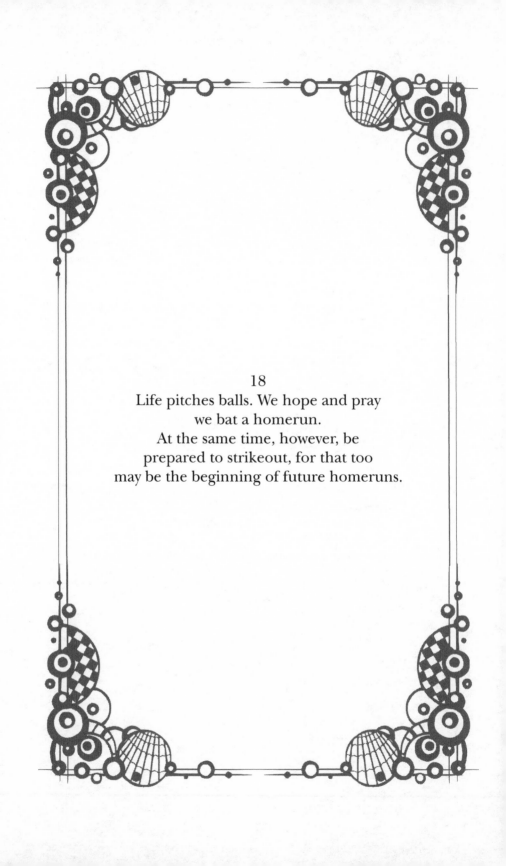

18
Life pitches balls. We hope and pray
we bat a homerun.
At the same time, however, be
prepared to strikeout, for that too
may be the beginning of future homeruns.

19
Your single most valuable mentor is
your life experiences.

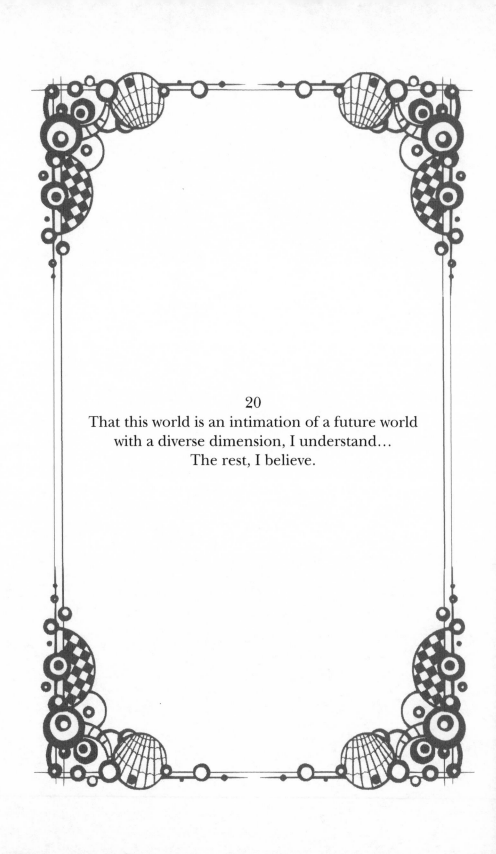

20
That this world is an intimation of a future world
with a diverse dimension, I understand…
The rest, I believe.

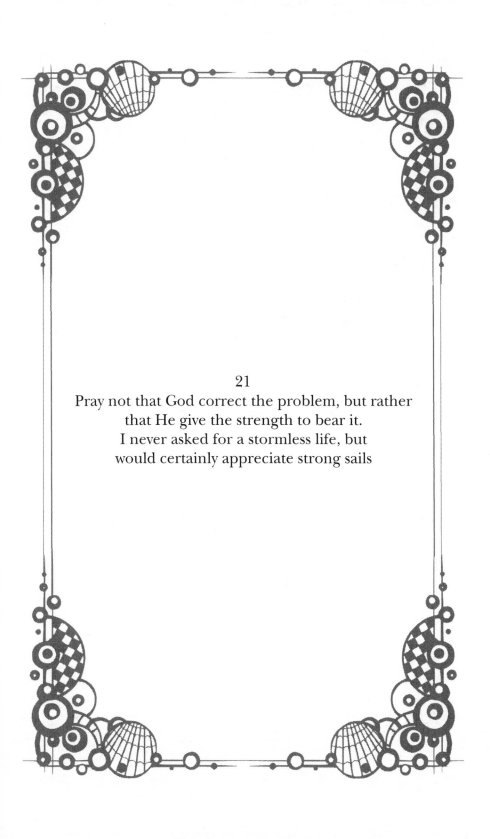

21
Pray not that God correct the problem, but rather
that He give the strength to bear it.
I never asked for a stormless life, but
would certainly appreciate strong sails

22
True and everlasting love is the
intimacy of two minds…
The rest is infatuation.

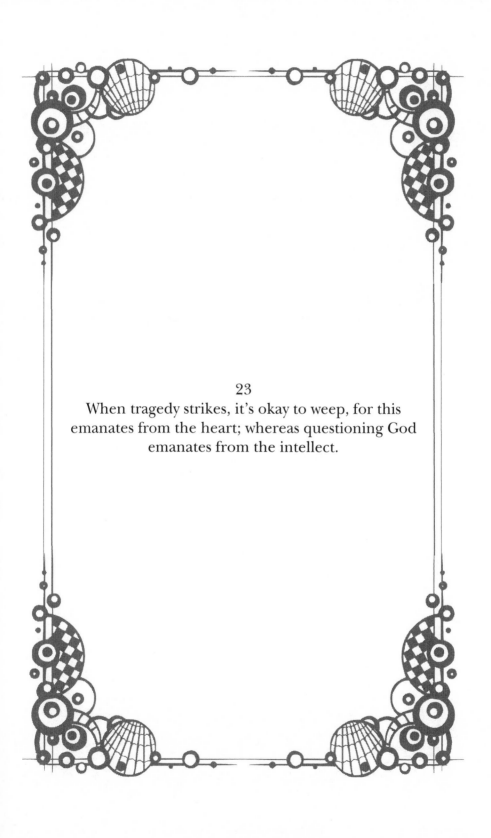

23
When tragedy strikes, it's okay to weep, for this
emanates from the heart; whereas questioning God
emanates from the intellect.

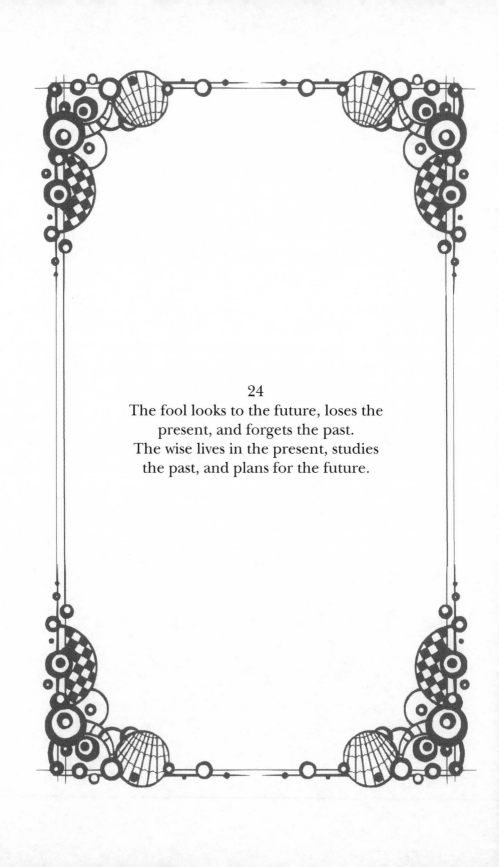

24
The fool looks to the future, loses the
present, and forgets the past.
The wise lives in the present, studies
the past, and plans for the future.

25
<u>Blind faith vs. Seeing faith.</u>
One must first "see", so that one may have faith in
that which one does not.

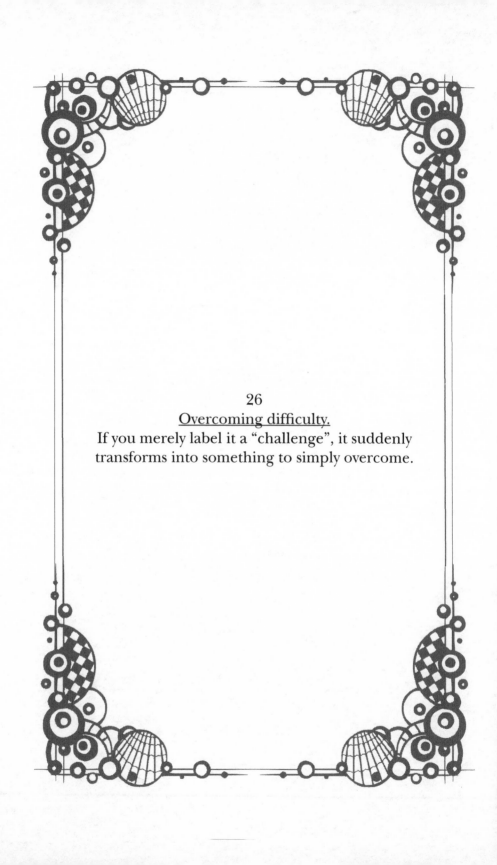

26
<u>Overcoming difficulty.</u>
If you merely label it a "challenge", it suddenly
transforms into something to simply overcome.

27

It's not how the world treats you, as much as
how you *perceive* the world treats you.

28
Don't confuse humility with low self esteem.
Recognize the good and potential
within you and be proud of it.

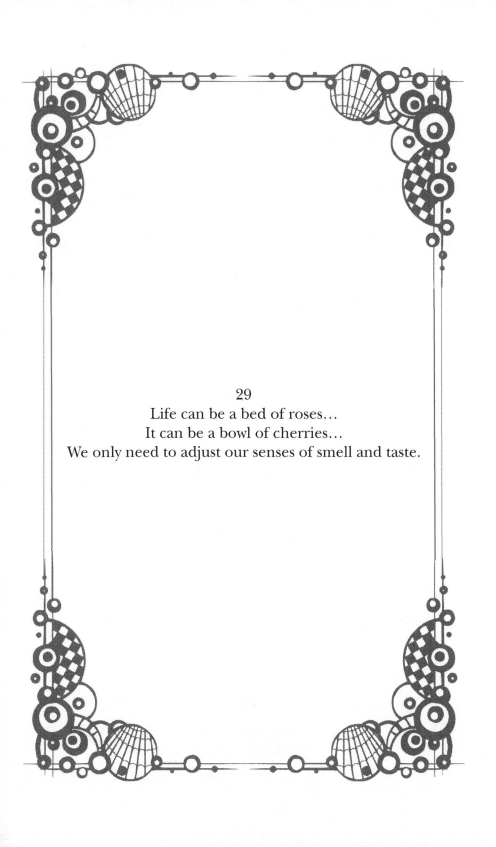

29
Life can be a bed of roses…
It can be a bowl of cherries…
We only need to adjust our senses of smell and taste.

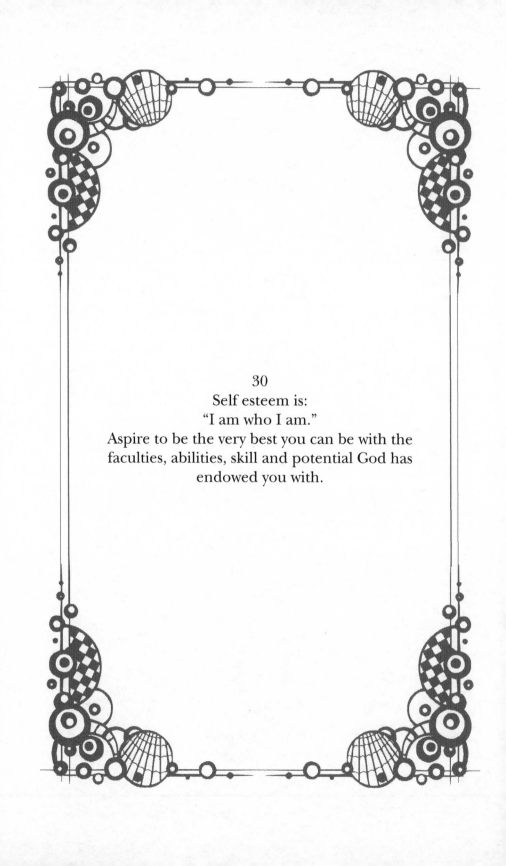

30
Self esteem is:
"I am who I am."
Aspire to be the very best you can be with the
faculties, abilities, skill and potential God has
endowed you with.

31
Plan to live to age 120.
Be prepared, though, to exit earlier.

32
One can choose to be afraid of the unknown,
or challenged by it.

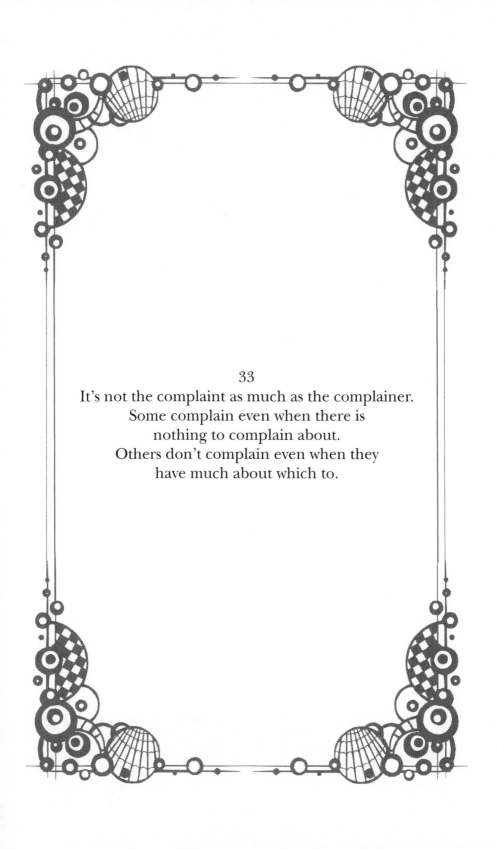

33
It's not the complaint as much as the complainer.
Some complain even when there is
nothing to complain about.
Others don't complain even when they
have much about which to.

34
By having a "purpose" in life, one can
overcome its "difficulties".

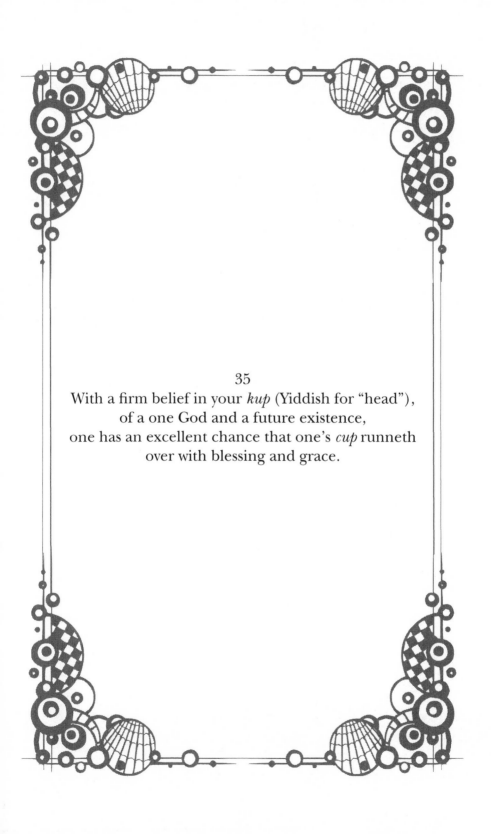

35
With a firm belief in your *kup* (Yiddish for "head"),
of a one God and a future existence,
one has an excellent chance that one's *cup* runneth
over with blessing and grace.

36
Contemplate for a moment, and see how many of
your problems are really self induced.

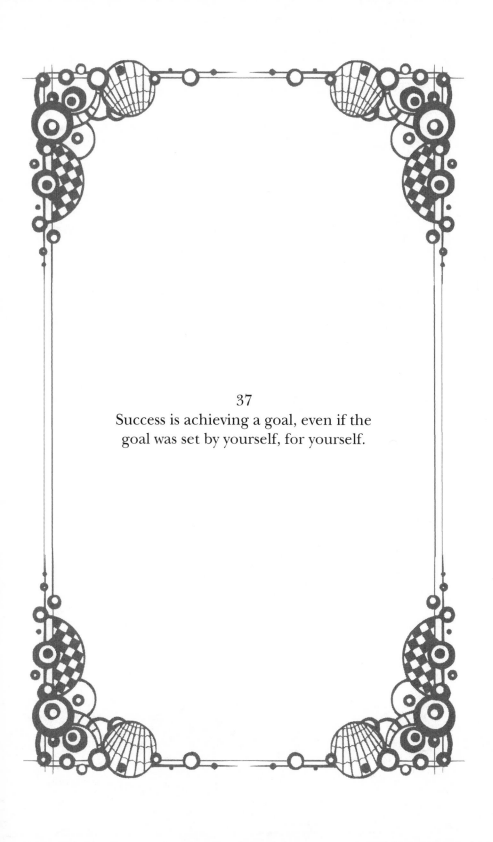

37
Success is achieving a goal, even if the
goal was set by yourself, for yourself.

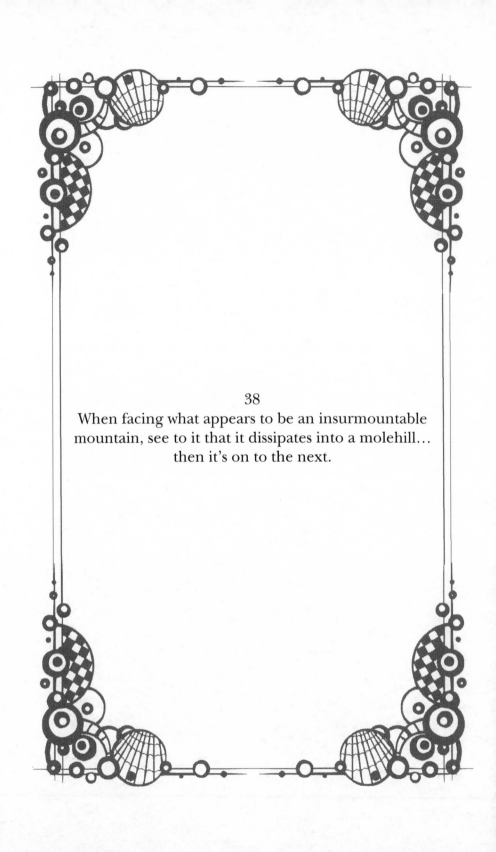

38
When facing what appears to be an insurmountable
mountain, see to it that it dissipates into a molehill...
then it's on to the next.

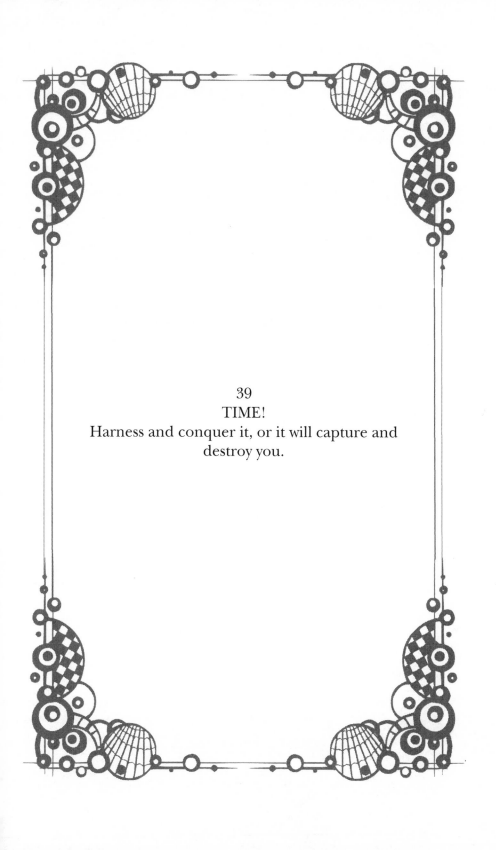

39
TIME!
Harness and conquer it, or it will capture and
destroy you.

40
Extremism is not how deeply one's convictions about a certain ideology are, but rather the way in which one attempts to persuade others of them.

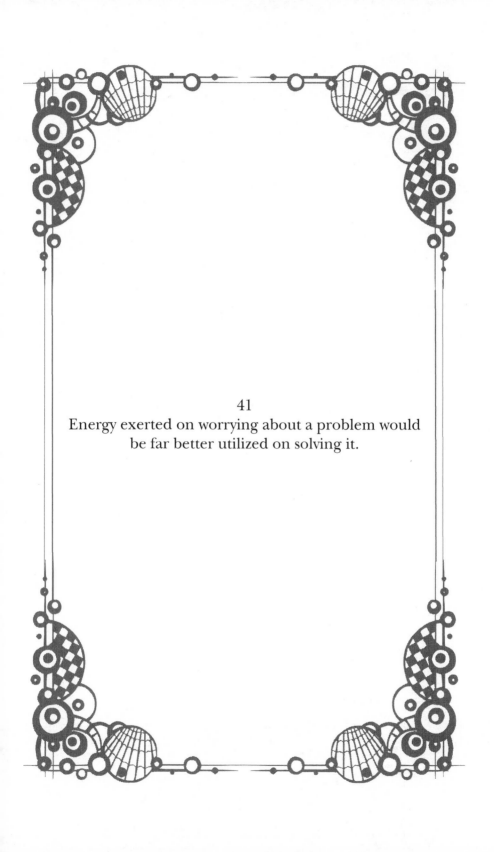

41
Energy exerted on worrying about a problem would
be far better utilized on solving it.

42

Sometimes, in the darkest hour of tragedy, we find the light of salvation.

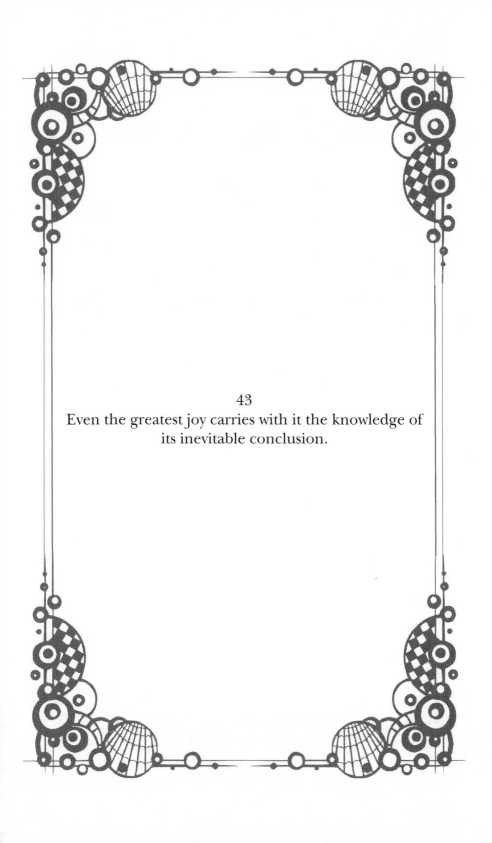

43

Even the greatest joy carries with it the knowledge of
its inevitable conclusion.

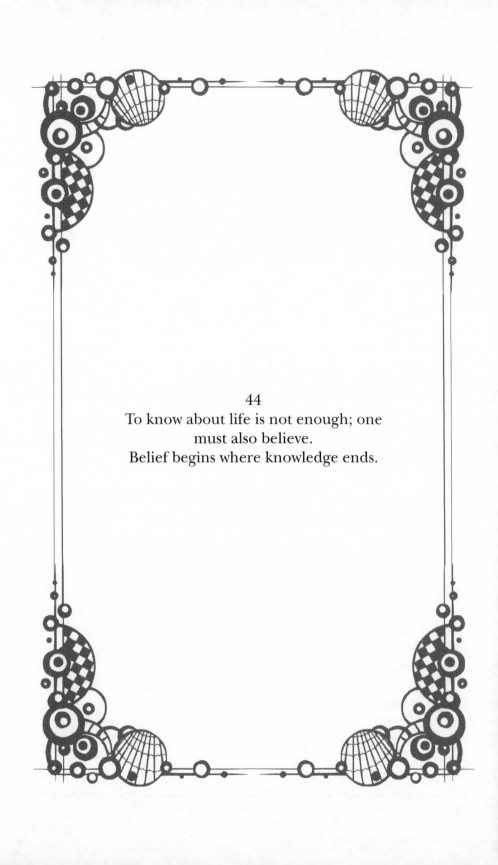

44
To know about life is not enough; one
must also believe.
Belief begins where knowledge ends.

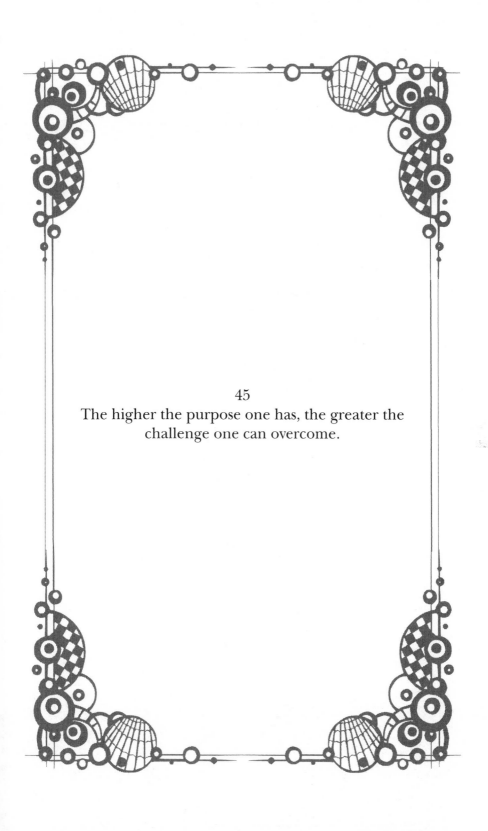

45
The higher the purpose one has, the greater the
challenge one can overcome.

46
In 1996, when the East Coast got clobbered with the
third worst winter storm in recorded history,
some in the Northwest were complaining about a
weather forecast predicting 2-4 inches.
Were you one of them?

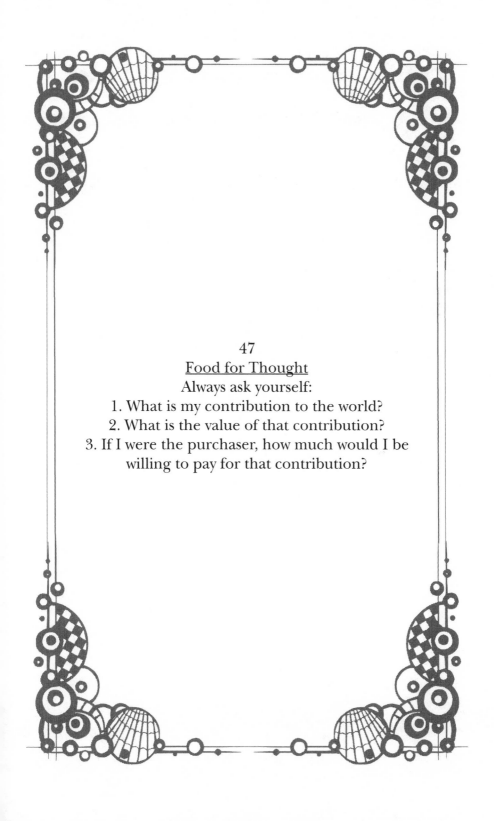

47
<u>Food for Thought</u>
Always ask yourself:
1. What is my contribution to the world?
2. What is the value of that contribution?
3. If I were the purchaser, how much would I be
   willing to pay for that contribution?

48
Thank goodness for the weather…
It keeps the complaining personality
busy all year round.

49

There is a big difference between *saying* thank you
and *being* thankful.

50

The crutches of blame and excuse accomplish
absolutely nothing, other than to stymie and stunt
the growth of one's character and eventual success.

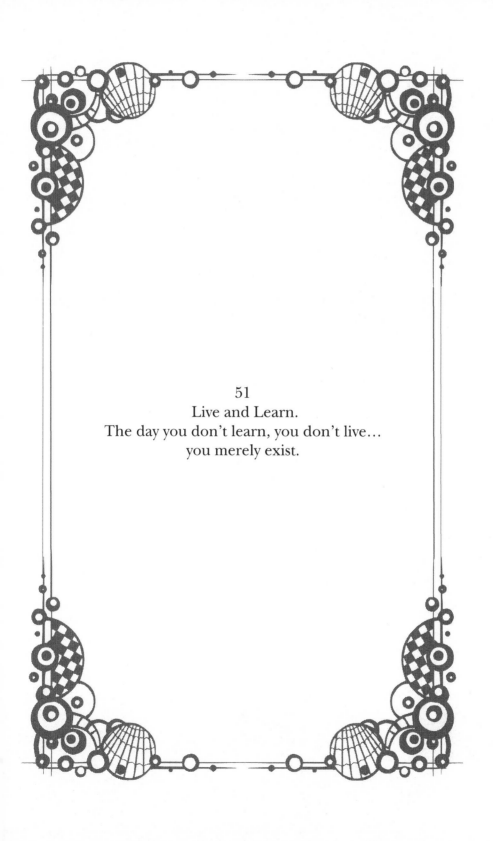

51
Live and Learn.
The day you don't learn, you don't live...
you merely exist.

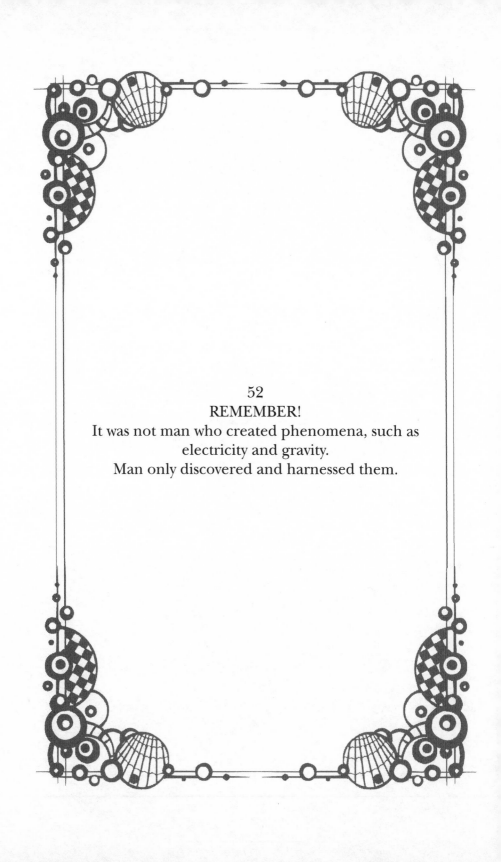

52
REMEMBER!
It was not man who created phenomena, such as
electricity and gravity.
Man only discovered and harnessed them.

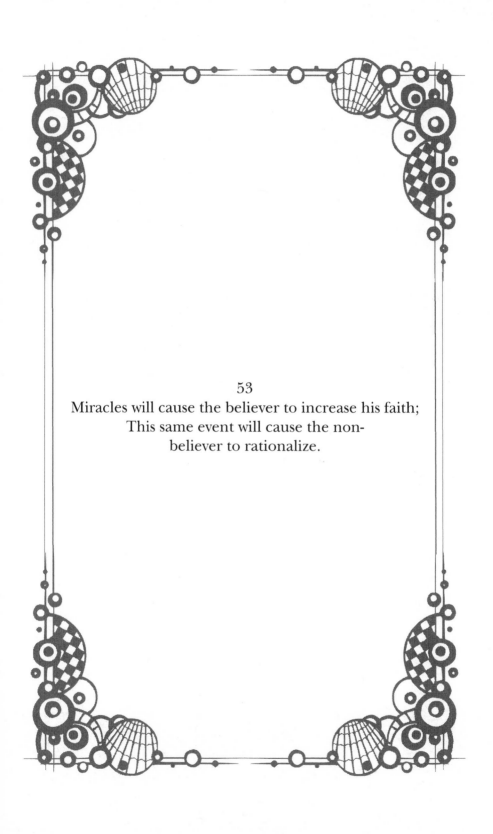

53
Miracles will cause the believer to increase his faith;
This same event will cause the non-
believer to rationalize.

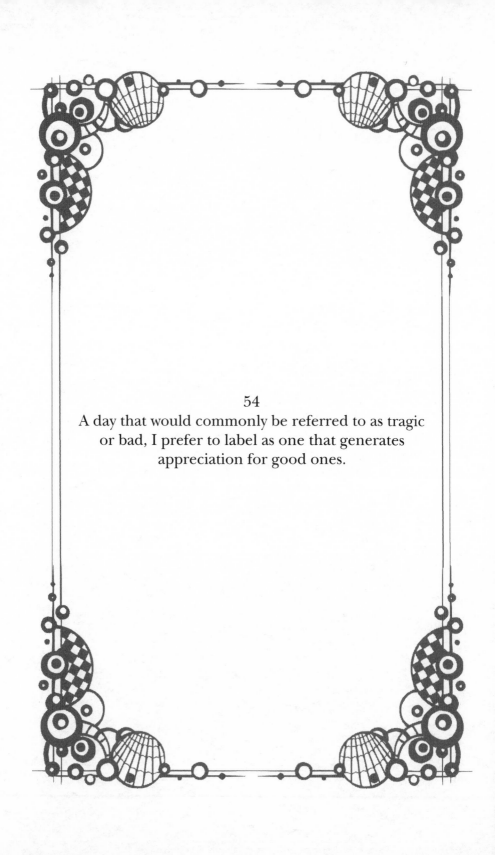

54
A day that would commonly be referred to as tragic
or bad, I prefer to label as one that generates
appreciation for good ones.

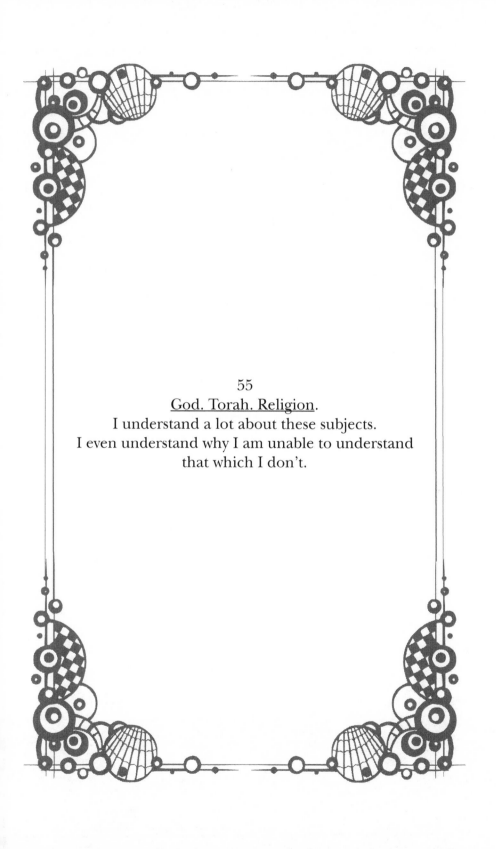

55
<u>God. Torah. Religion</u>.
I understand a lot about these subjects.
I even understand why I am unable to understand
that which I don't.

56
There is no Reality.
There is, however, optimism and pessimism...
It all depends on the beholder's perception.

57
Modification is the bridge that
connects fantasy with reality.

58
If one's word is not his bond, then
neither will his oath or signature be.
(I learned this maxim the hard way!)

59
It's bad enough that this thing
(whatever the thing may be) happened to me;
I have resolved not to make it even
worse by getting aggravated over it.

60
If you don't stop to *think*, you will never *thank*.

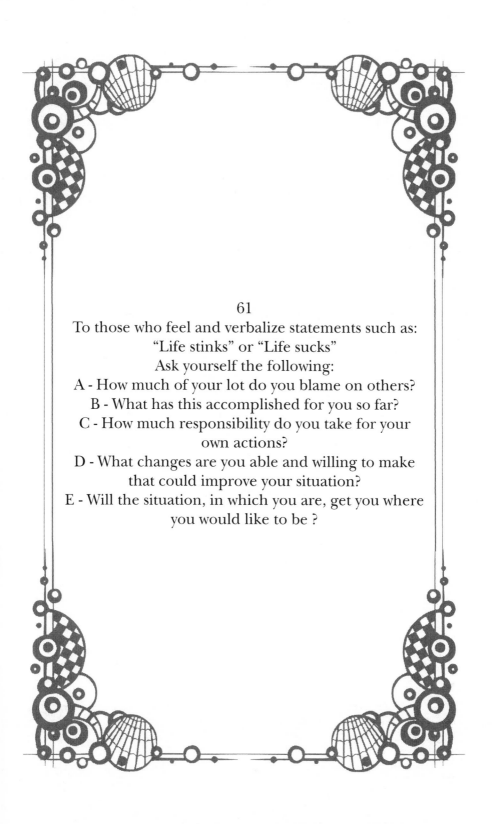

61

To those who feel and verbalize statements such as:
"Life stinks" or "Life sucks"
Ask yourself the following:

A - How much of your lot do you blame on others?

B - What has this accomplished for you so far?

C - How much responsibility do you take for your own actions?

D - What changes are you able and willing to make that could improve your situation?

E - Will the situation, in which you are, get you where you would like to be ?

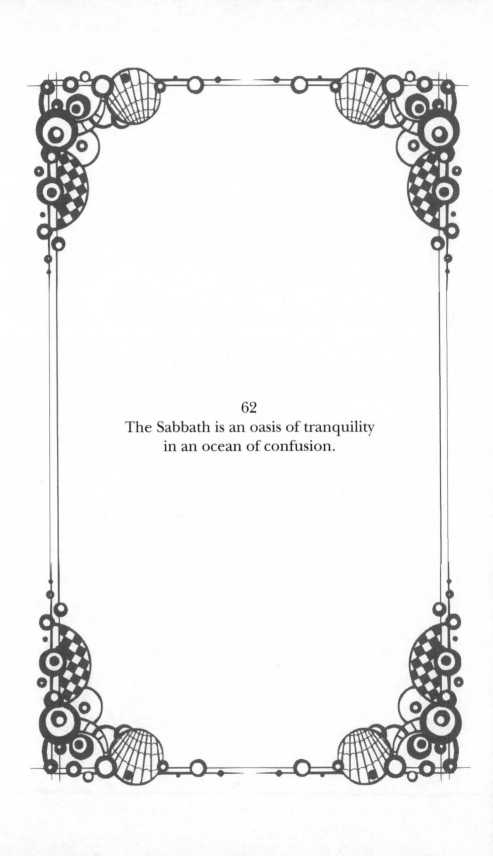

62
The Sabbath is an oasis of tranquility
in an ocean of confusion.

63
True friendship is not permitting a
disagreement to escalate into war.

64
The rules of life are the same as those
for the electrician.
You're entitled to mistakes, but, like an
electrician, some are fatal!

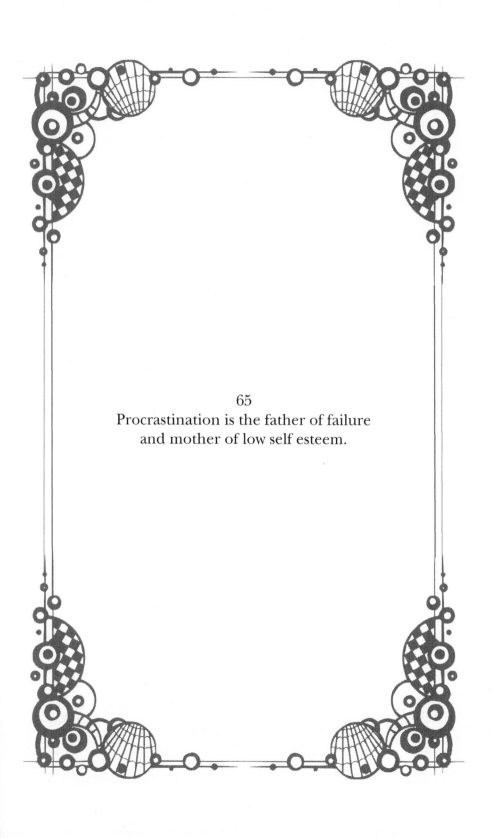

65
Procrastination is the father of failure
and mother of low self esteem.

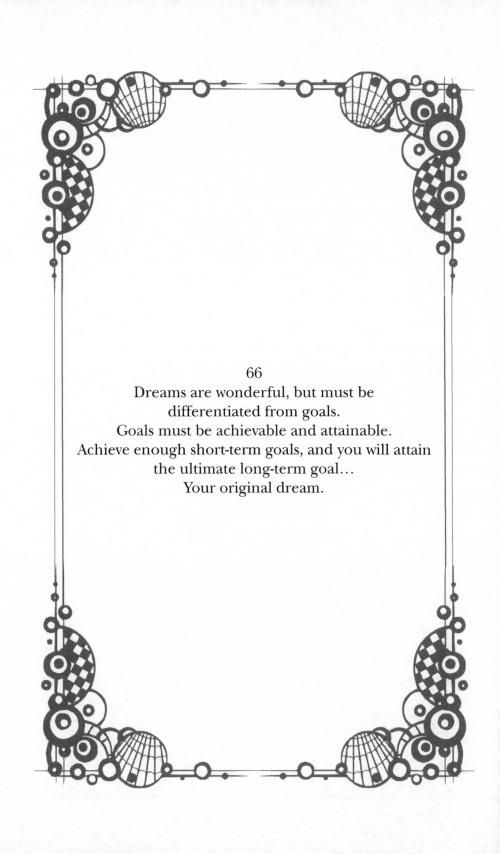

66
Dreams are wonderful, but must be
differentiated from goals.
Goals must be achievable and attainable.
Achieve enough short-term goals, and you will attain
the ultimate long-term goal...
Your original dream.

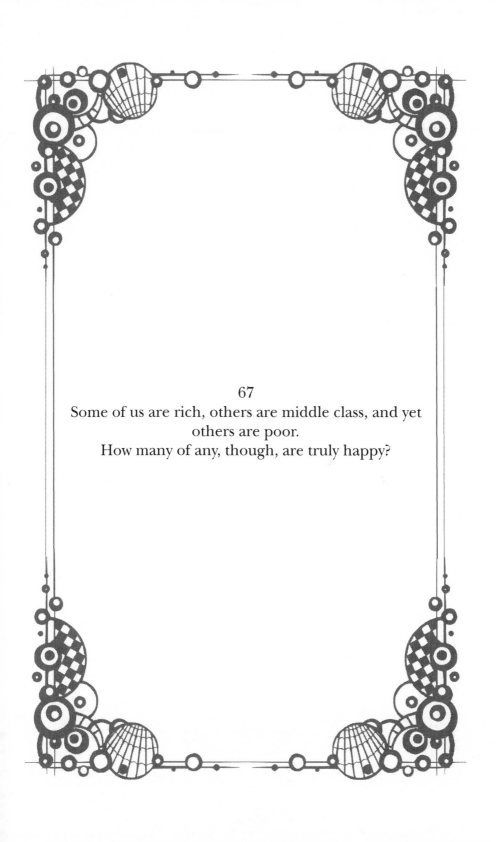

67

Some of us are rich, others are middle class, and yet
others are poor.
How many of any, though, are truly happy?

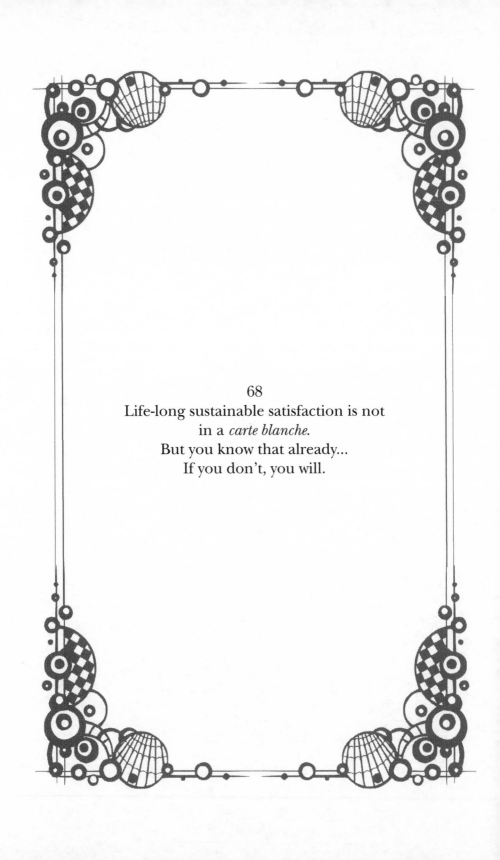

68
Life-long sustainable satisfaction is not
in a *carte blanche.*
But you know that already...
If you don't, you will.

69

To find happiness, focus on the good
in everything and everybody.
Focusing on the opposite, will result in the opposite.
Because in the illustrious words of Henry Ford:
Whether you think you can or you can't, you're right.

70
Every day a new sunrise.

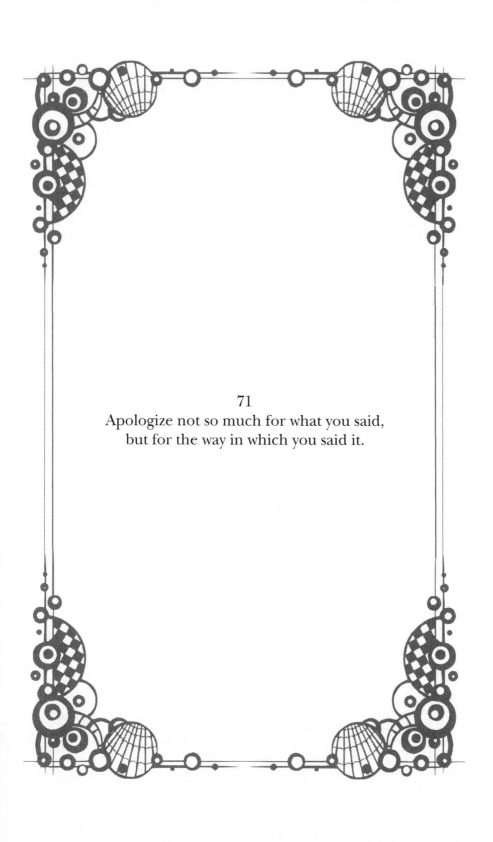

71
Apologize not so much for what you said,
but for the way in which you said it.

72
Focusing on the goal, makes the
getting there much easier.

73
With a positive attitude, one is able to
overcome life's greatest obstacles.

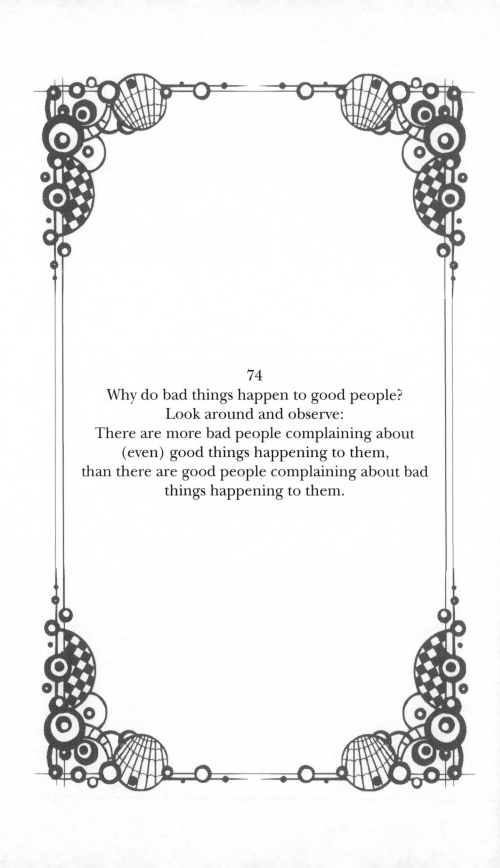

74
Why do bad things happen to good people?
Look around and observe:
There are more bad people complaining about
(even) good things happening to them,
than there are good people complaining about bad
things happening to them.

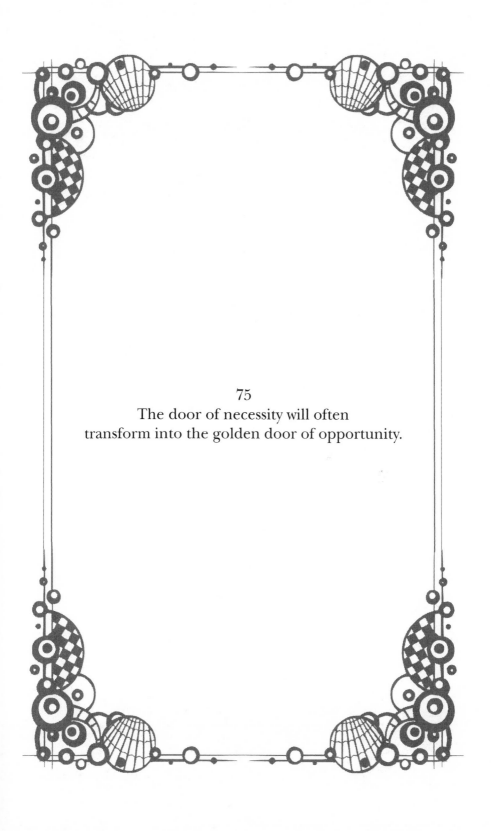

75
The door of necessity will often
transform into the golden door of opportunity.

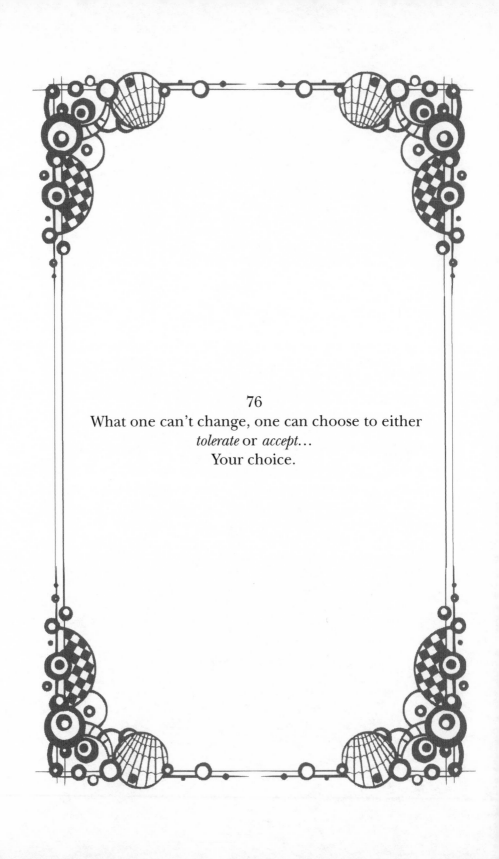

76
What one can't change, one can choose to either
tolerate or *accept*...
Your choice.

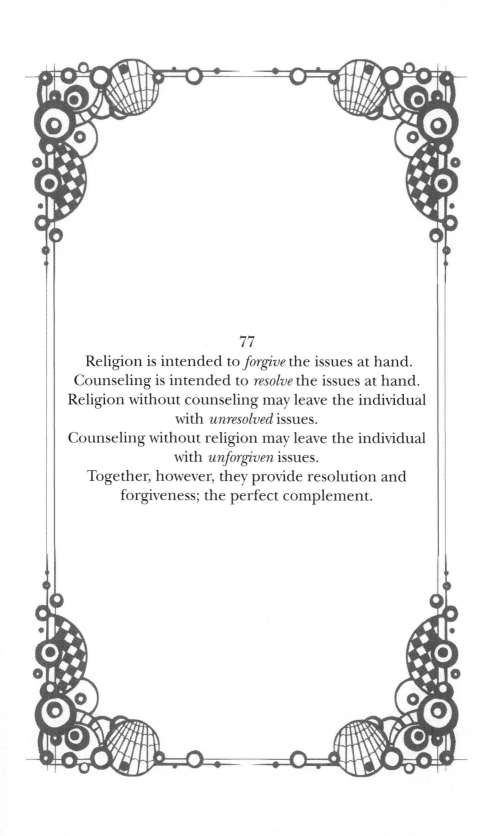

77

Religion is intended to *forgive* the issues at hand.
Counseling is intended to *resolve* the issues at hand.
Religion without counseling may leave the individual
with *unresolved* issues.
Counseling without religion may leave the individual
with *unforgiven* issues.
Together, however, they provide resolution and
forgiveness; the perfect complement.

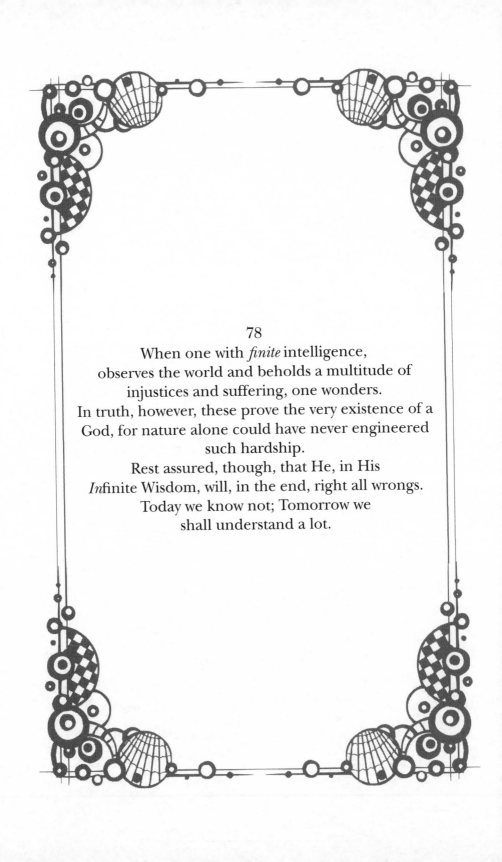

78

When one with *finite* intelligence,
observes the world and beholds a multitude of
injustices and suffering, one wonders.
In truth, however, these prove the very existence of a
God, for nature alone could have never engineered
such hardship.
Rest assured, though, that He, in His
*In*finite Wisdom, will, in the end, right all wrongs.
Today we know not; Tomorrow we
shall understand a lot.

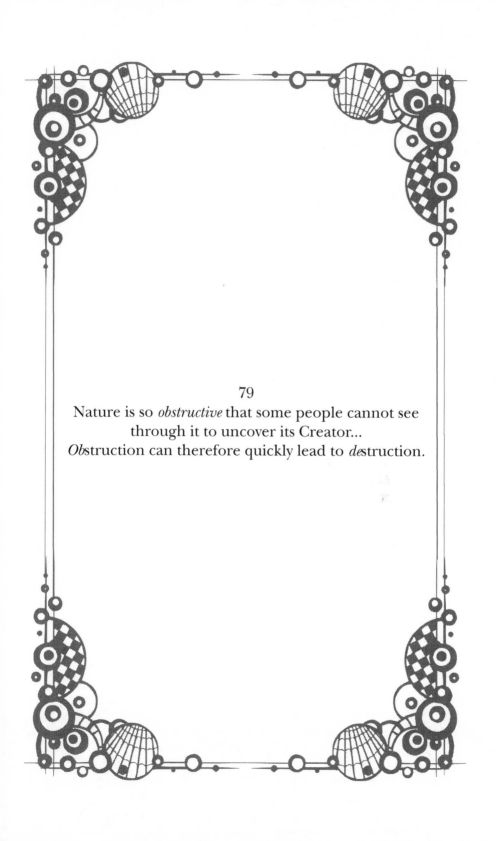

79

Nature is so *obstructive* that some people cannot see
through it to uncover its Creator...
*Ob*struction can therefore quickly lead to *de*struction.

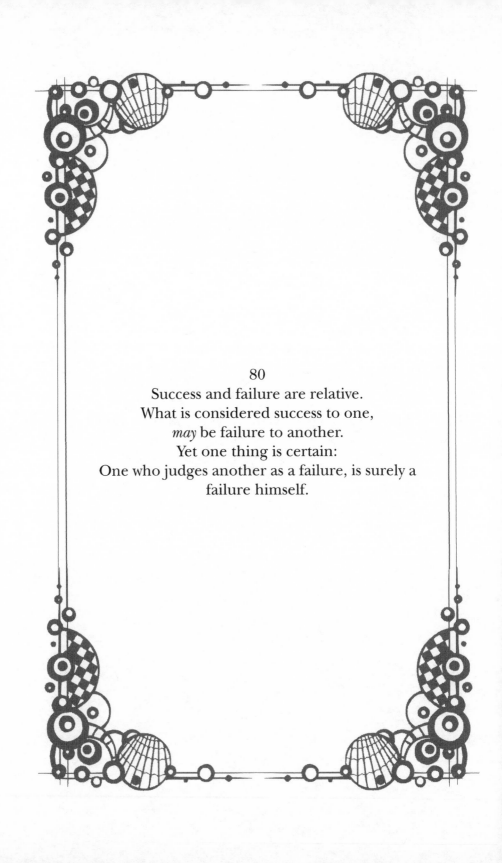

80
Success and failure are relative.
What is considered success to one,
may be failure to another.
Yet one thing is certain:
One who judges another as a failure, is surely a
failure himself.

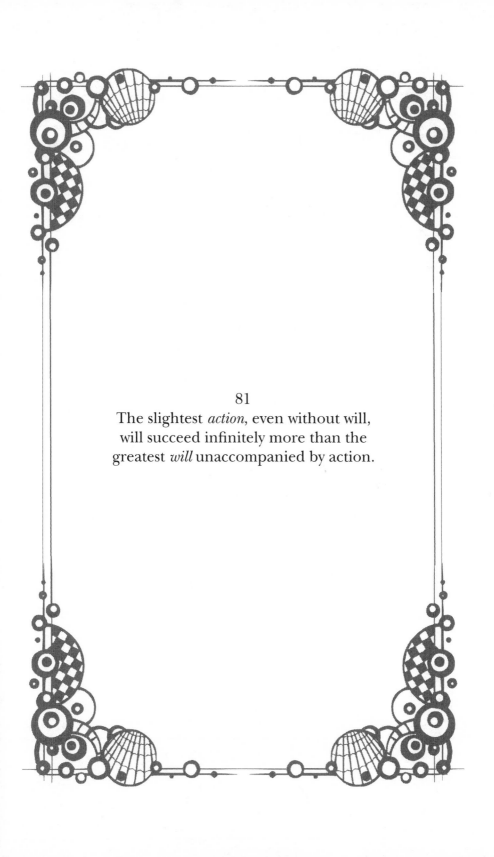

81
The slightest *action*, even without will,
will succeed infinitely more than the
greatest *will* unaccompanied by action.

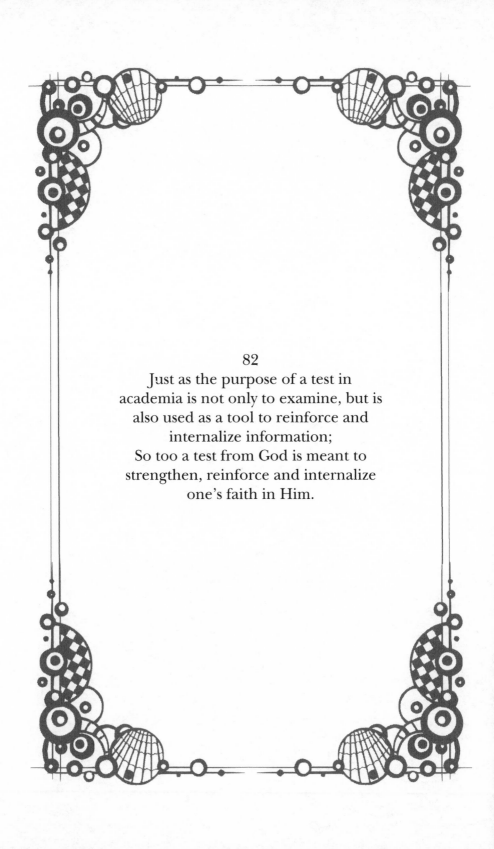

82

Just as the purpose of a test in academia is not only to examine, but is also used as a tool to reinforce and internalize information;
So too a test from God is meant to strengthen, reinforce and internalize one's faith in Him.

83
If life were stripped of challenges, life
would be *truly* challenging.

84
I cannot help growing old, but I can
strive to remain young.

85
On time, is late!

86
Ups and downs are relative.
The terminally ill patient would have a surging up
day if his only ill were the investor's down day.

87
When the patient says:
I can't talk about it or *I am not a
talker,* he has spoken greater volumes
than had he actually said anything at all.

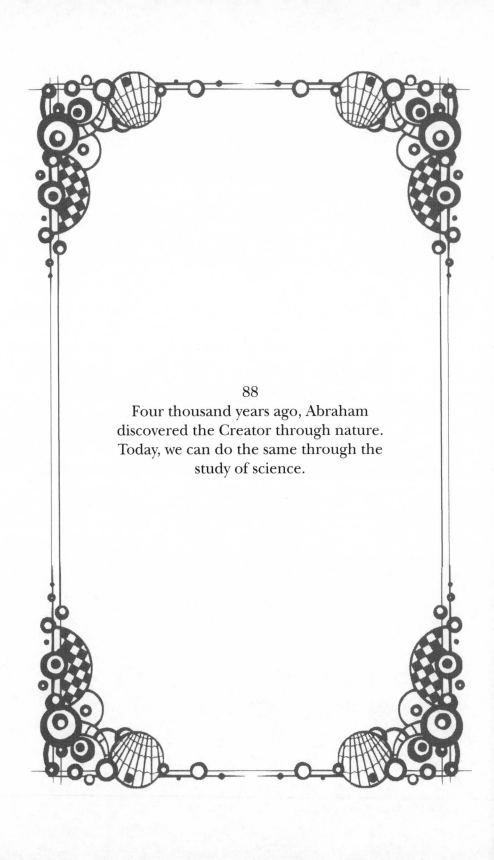

88
Four thousand years ago, Abraham
discovered the Creator through nature.
Today, we can do the same through the
study of science.

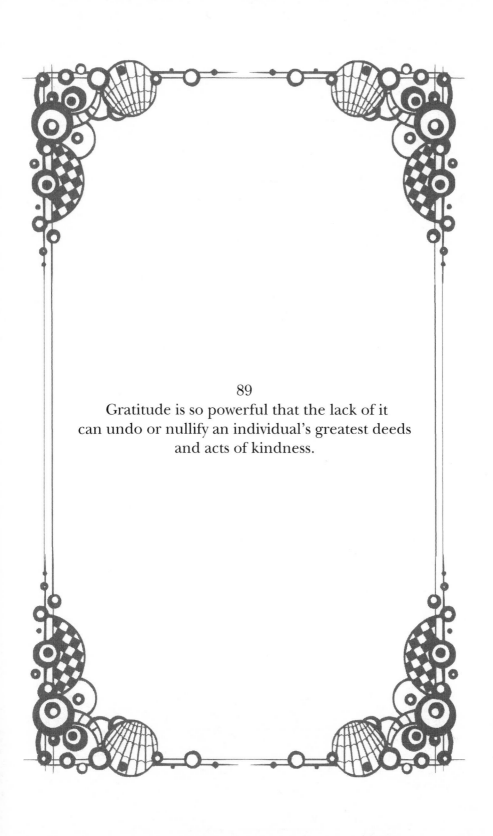

89
Gratitude is so powerful that the lack of it
can undo or nullify an individual's greatest deeds
and acts of kindness.

90
Not all hurting words are meant to be hurt*ful.*

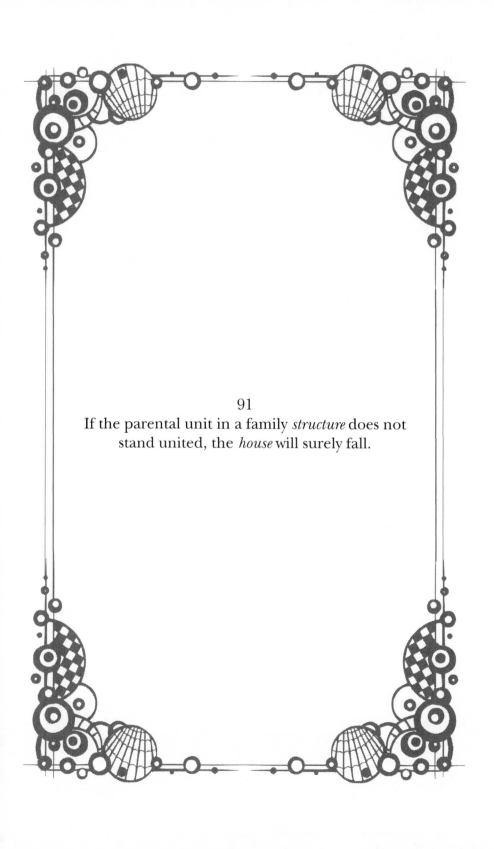

91

If the parental unit in a family *structure* does not
stand united, the *house* will surely fall.

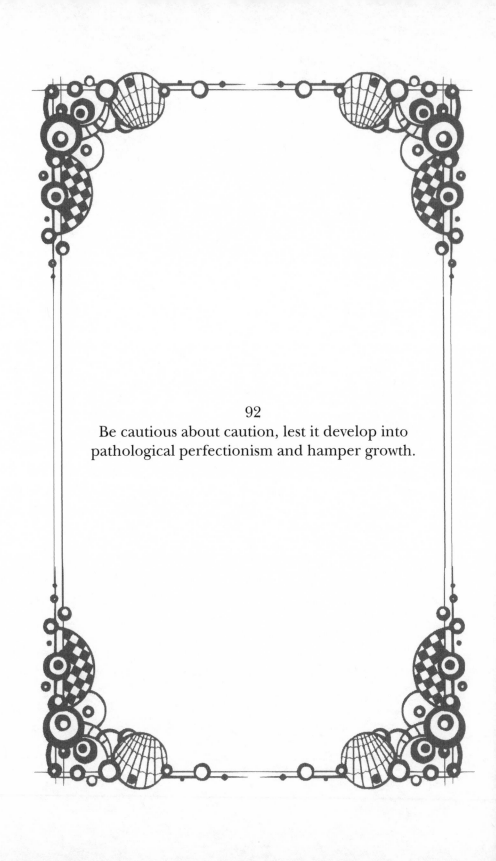

92
Be cautious about caution, lest it develop into
pathological perfectionism and hamper growth.

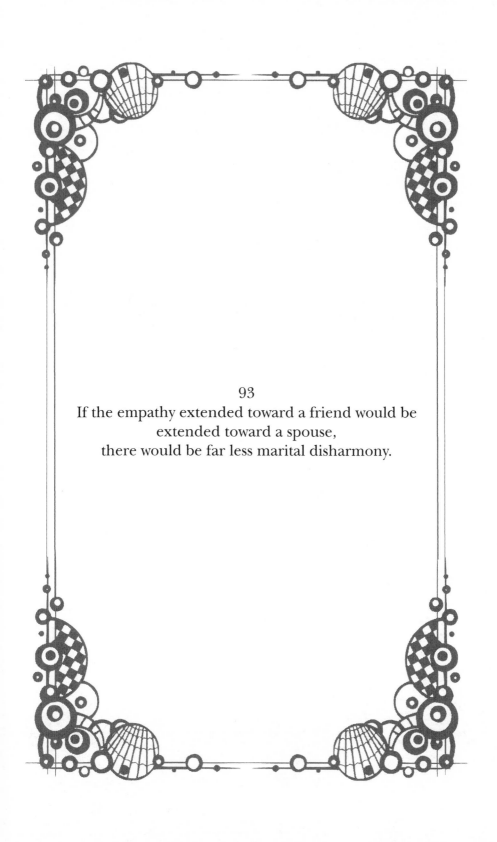

93
If the empathy extended toward a friend would be
extended toward a spouse,
there would be far less marital disharmony.

94
Worse than failure is the devastation
that accompanies it...
if you allow it to.

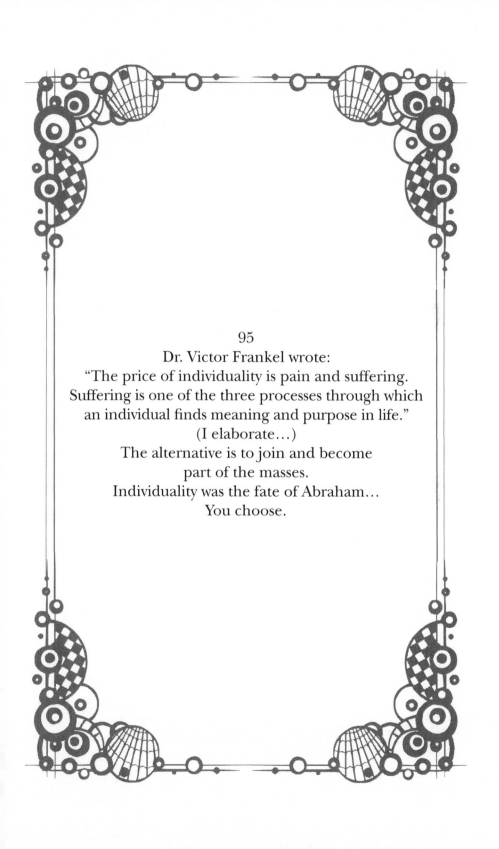

95
Dr. Victor Frankel wrote:
"The price of individuality is pain and suffering.
Suffering is one of the three processes through which
an individual finds meaning and purpose in life."
(I elaborate…)
The alternative is to join and become
part of the masses.
Individuality was the fate of Abraham…
You choose.

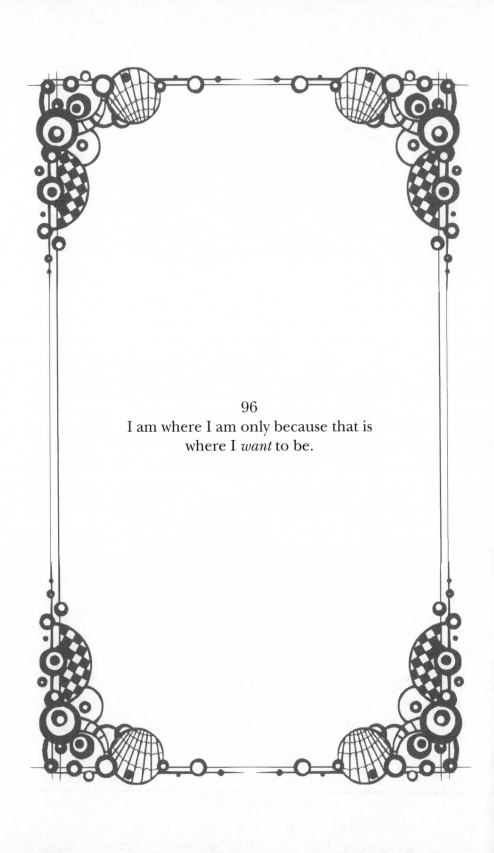

96
I am where I am only because that is
where I *want* to be.

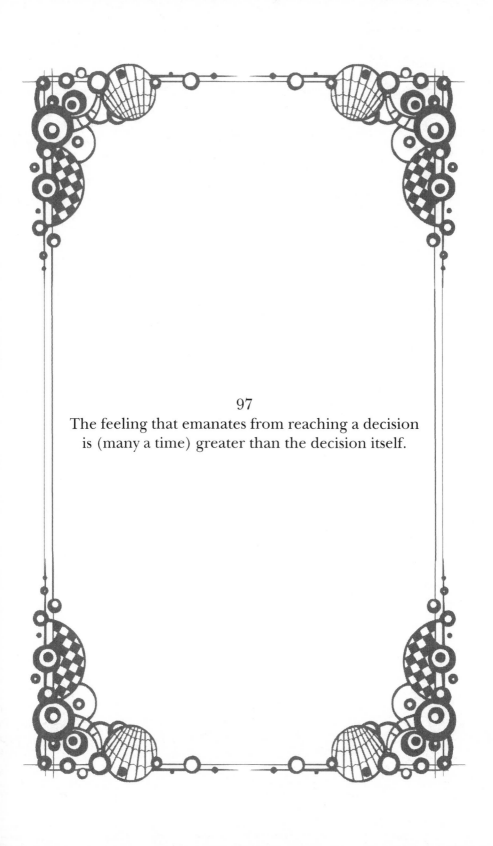

97
The feeling that emanates from reaching a decision
is (many a time) greater than the decision itself.

98
When I lose control over a situation,
my faith kicks in.
I place control in the hands of a *higher power*,
As a result, my angst dissipates.

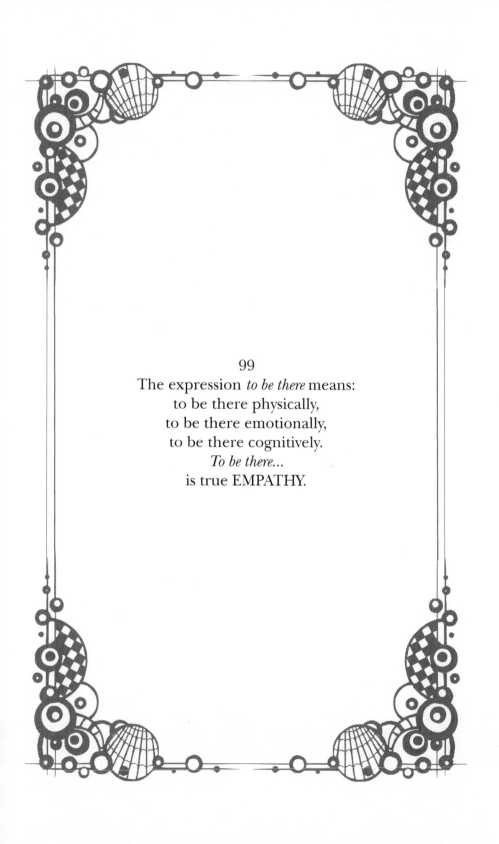

99

The expression *to be there* means:
to be there physically,
to be there emotionally,
to be there cognitively.
To be there...
is true EMPATHY.

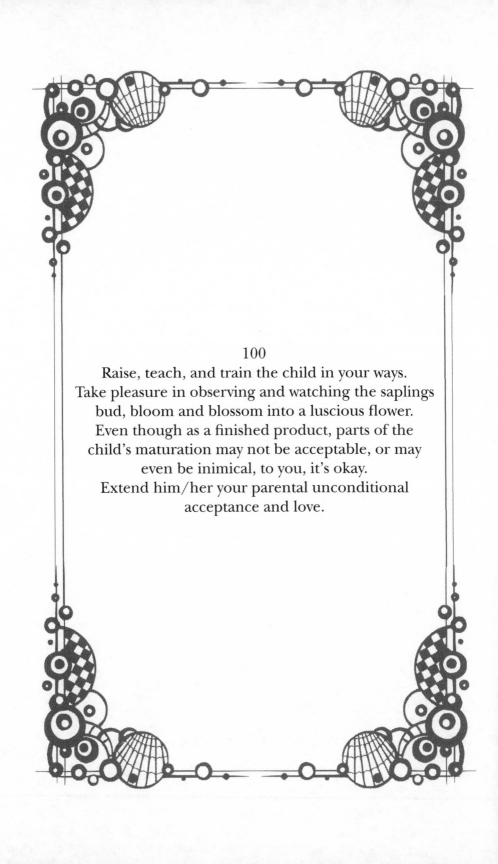

100

Raise, teach, and train the child in your ways.
Take pleasure in observing and watching the saplings
bud, bloom and blossom into a luscious flower.
Even though as a finished product, parts of the
child's maturation may not be acceptable, or may
even be inimical, to you, it's okay.
Extend him/her your parental unconditional
acceptance and love.

101
True communication is an art;
Art, though, is not a true form of communication.

102
True strength is in lifting oneself up after a fall –
Emotional or spiritual.

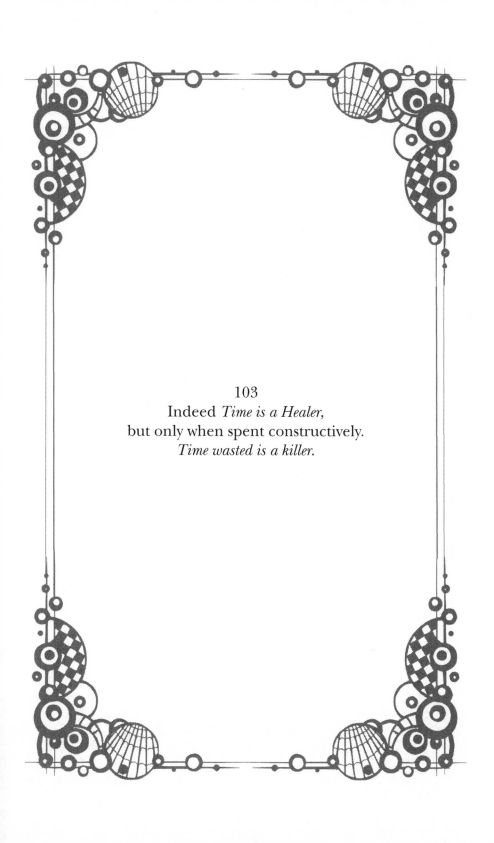

103
Indeed *Time is a Healer,*
but only when spent constructively.
Time wasted is a killer.

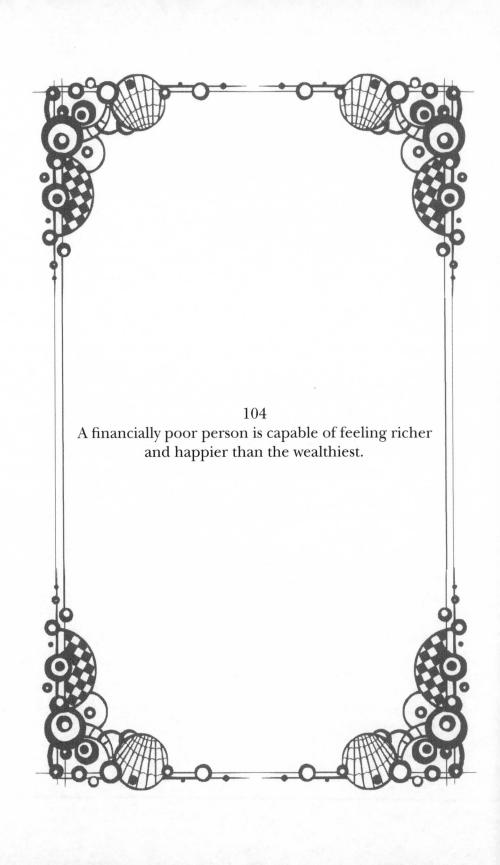

104
A financially poor person is capable of feeling richer
and happier than the wealthiest.

105
It is not the one who has, but the one who gives.

106
If having no money won't allow you to smile,
then *no* money will.

107
Sometimes, it is better to talk to a wall
than to another.

108
For the world to smile upon you, you must first smile upon it.

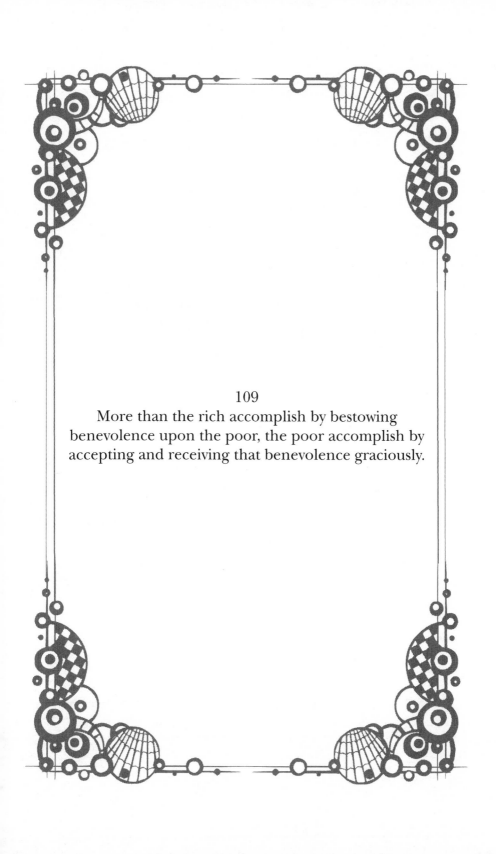

109

More than the rich accomplish by bestowing
benevolence upon the poor, the poor accomplish by
accepting and receiving that benevolence graciously.

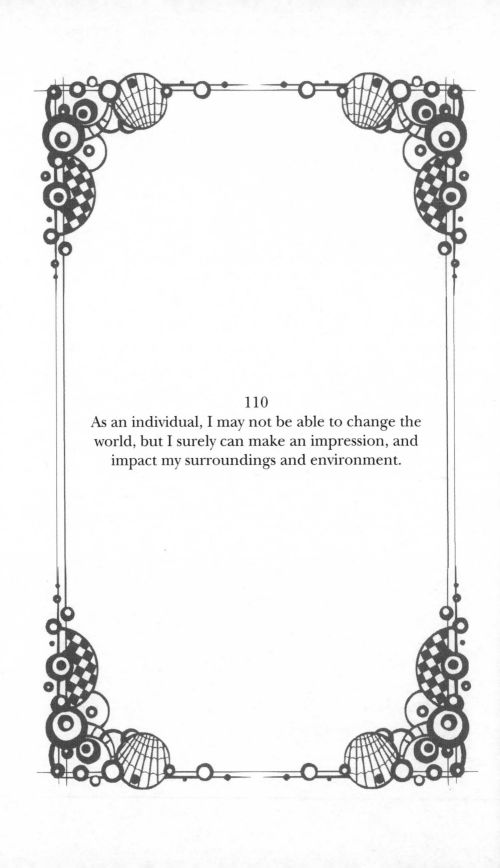

110
As an individual, I may not be able to change the
world, but I surely can make an impression, and
impact my surroundings and environment.

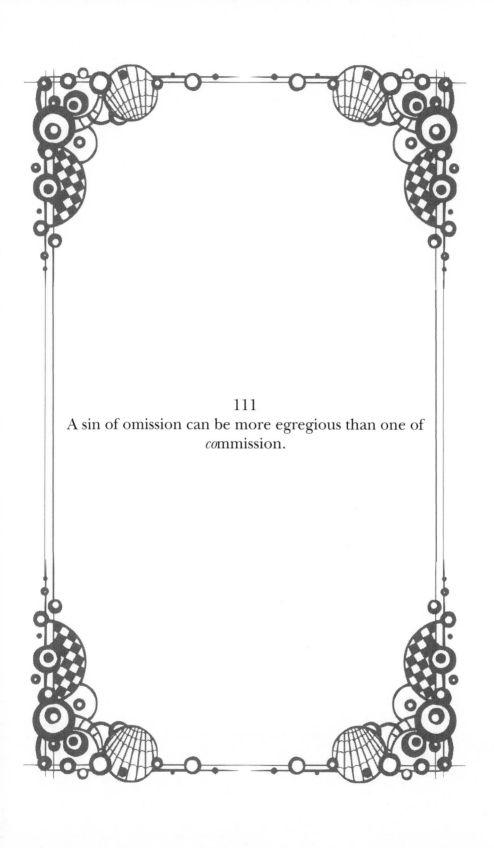

111

A sin of omission can be more egregious than one of *co*mmission.

112

Happiness is no *Mitzvah* (virtue), but what happiness
can achieve or lead to, no *Mitzvah* can;
Melancholy is no sin, but what melancholy can
achieve or lead to, no sin can.

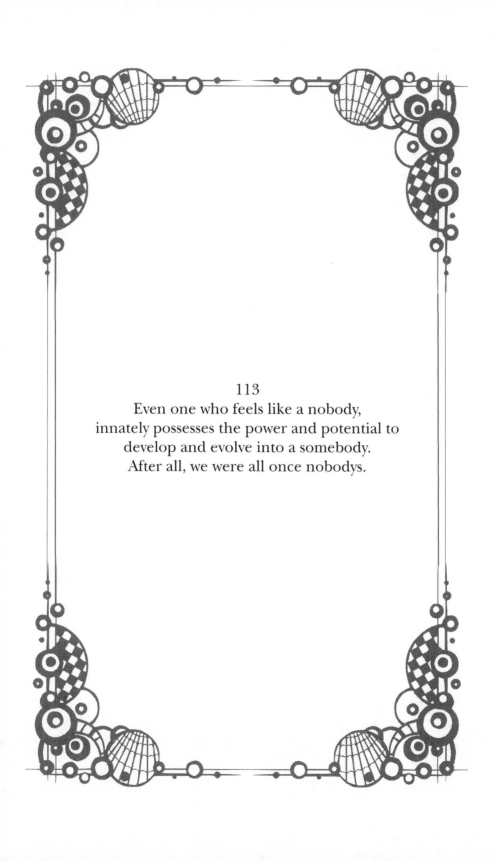

113

Even one who feels like a nobody,
innately possesses the power and potential to
develop and evolve into a somebody.
After all, we were all once nobodys.

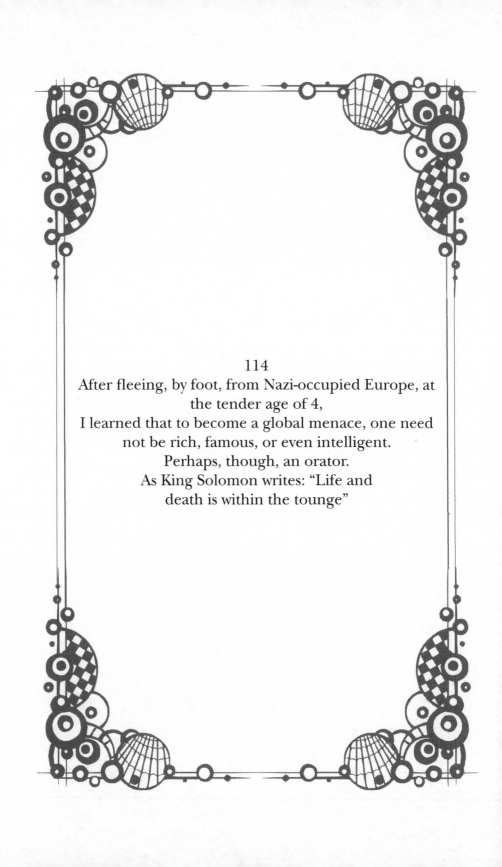

114

After fleeing, by foot, from Nazi-occupied Europe, at
the tender age of 4,
I learned that to become a global menace, one need
not be rich, famous, or even intelligent.
Perhaps, though, an orator.
As King Solomon writes: "Life and
death is within the tounge"

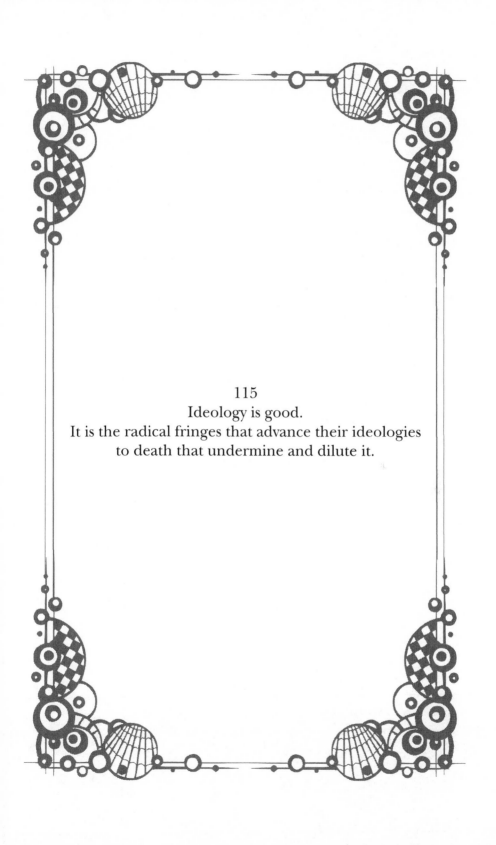

115
Ideology is good.
It is the radical fringes that advance their ideologies
to death that undermine and dilute it.

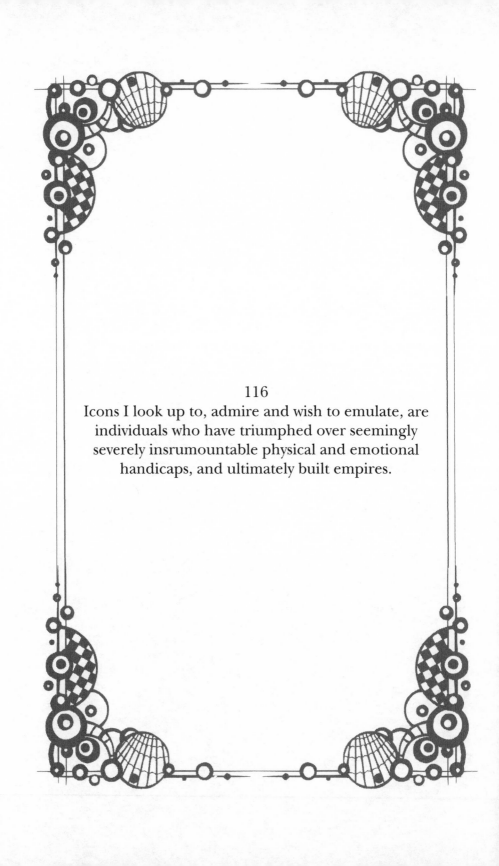

116
Icons I look up to, admire and wish to emulate, are
individuals who have triumphed over seemingly
severely insrumountable physical and emotional
handicaps, and ultimately built empires.

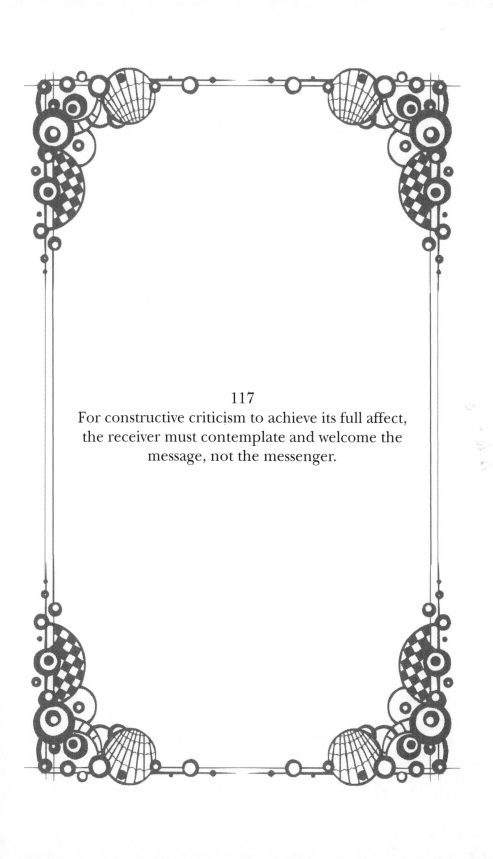

117
For constructive criticism to achieve its full affect,
the receiver must contemplate and welcome the
message, not the messenger.

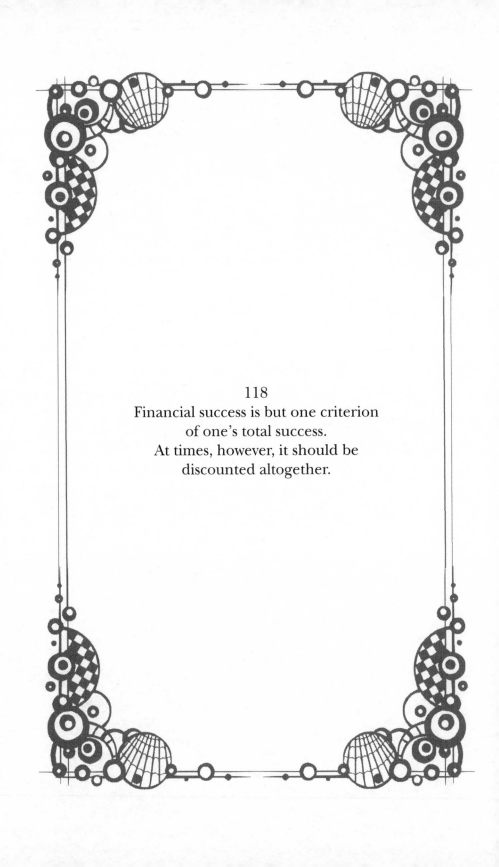

118
Financial success is but one criterion
of one's total success.
At times, however, it should be
discounted altogether.

119
Sleep is okay as a means of rest or relaxation, but not as an escape from life's reality and challenges.

120
The world to come is simply a continuing future
existence in a different dimension.

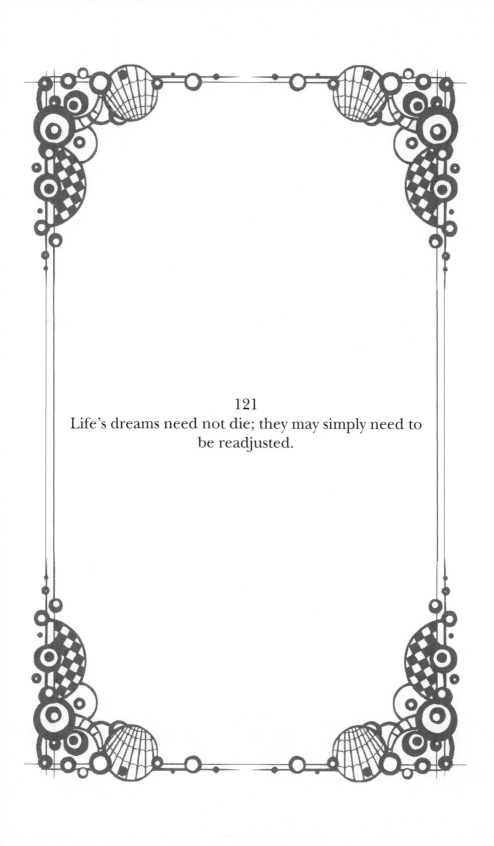

121
Life's dreams need not die; they may simply need to be readjusted.

122
Attire serves two opposite purposes:
It conceals the person,
and reveals the personality.

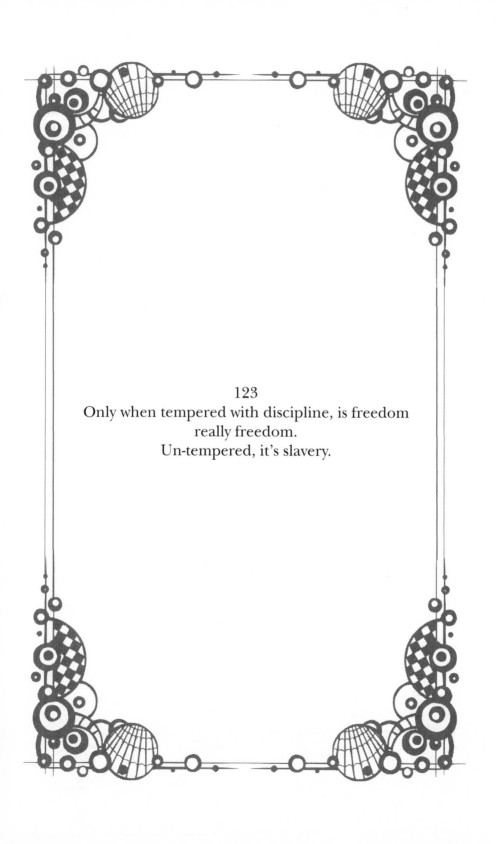

123
Only when tempered with discipline, is freedom
really freedom.
Un-tempered, it's slavery.

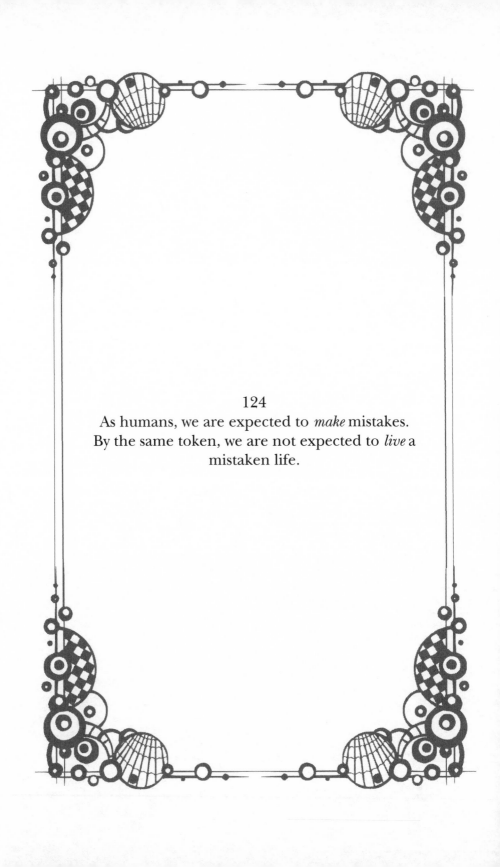

124
As humans, we are expected to *make* mistakes.
By the same token, we are not expected to *live* a
mistaken life.

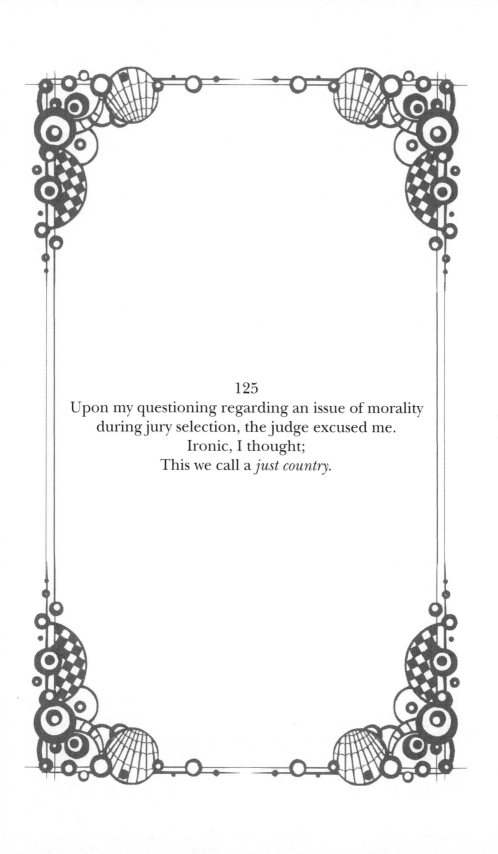

125

Upon my questioning regarding an issue of morality
during jury selection, the judge excused me.
Ironic, I thought;
This we call a *just country.*

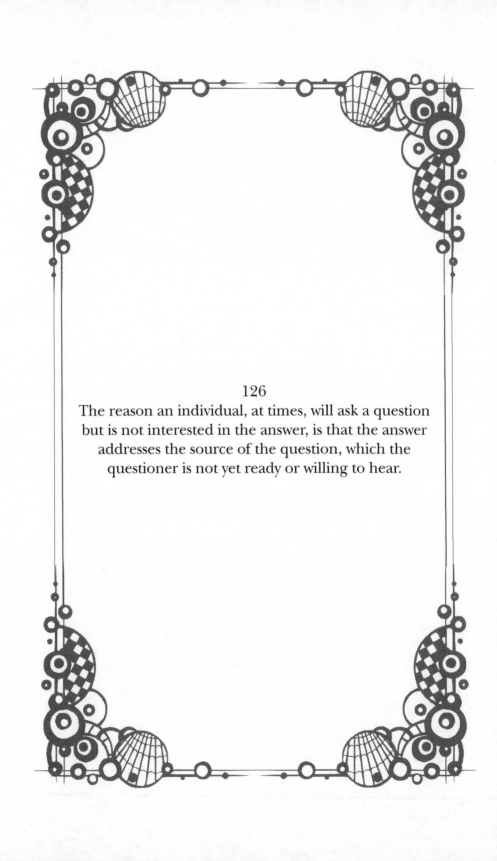

126

The reason an individual, at times, will ask a question but is not interested in the answer, is that the answer addresses the source of the question, which the questioner is not yet ready or willing to hear.

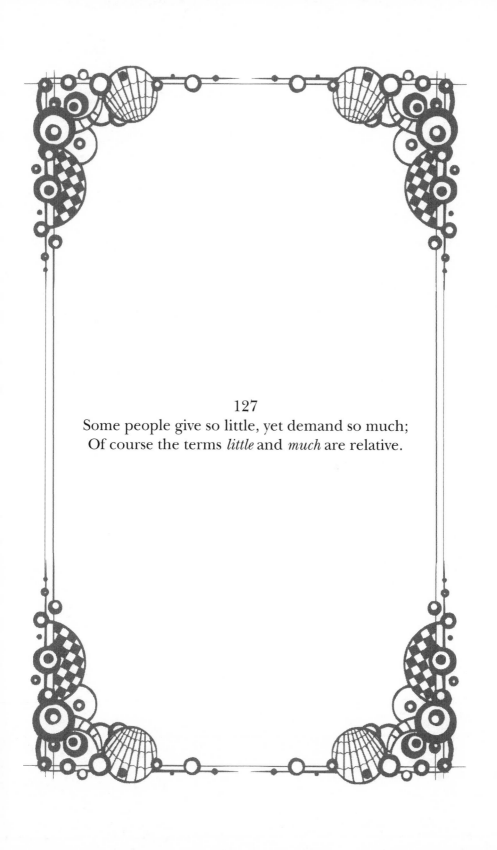

127
Some people give so little, yet demand so much;
Of course the terms *little* and *much* are relative.

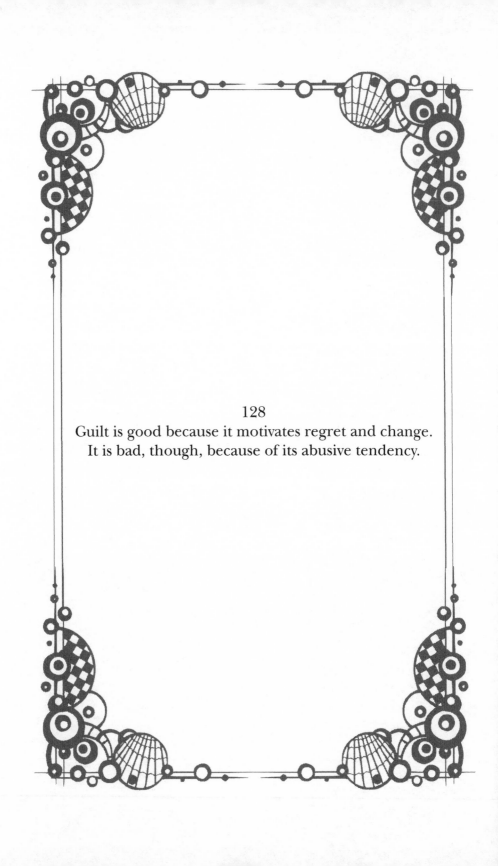

128
Guilt is good because it motivates regret and change.
It is bad, though, because of its abusive tendency.

129
More than love, the fabric that cements
marital relationships is:
Commitment, trust and respect.

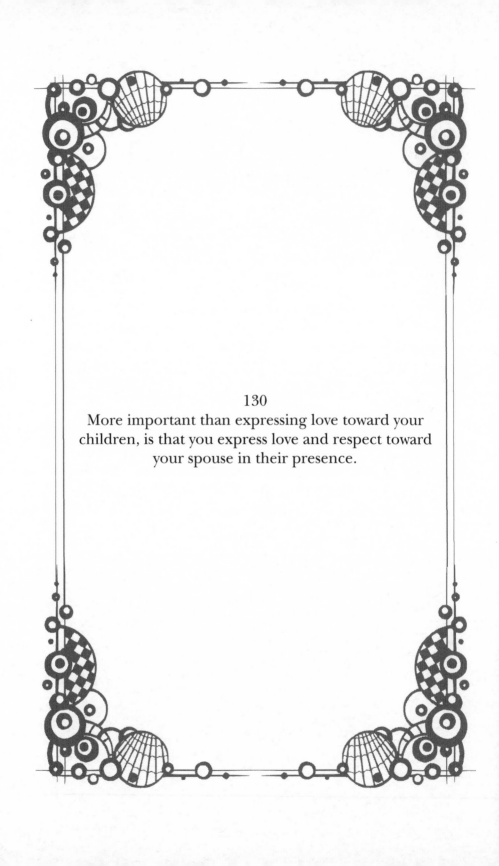

130
More important than expressing love toward your children, is that you express love and respect toward your spouse in their presence.

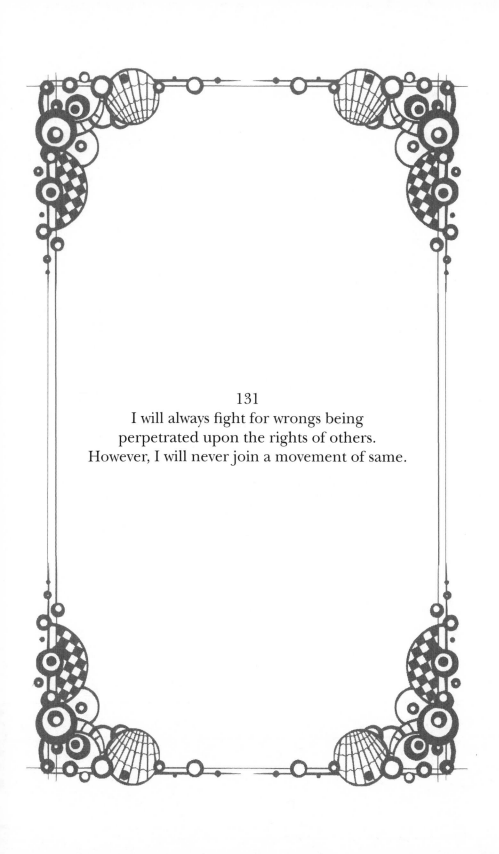

131
I will always fight for wrongs being
perpetrated upon the rights of others.
However, I will never join a movement of same.

132
When an intellectual disagreement descends into an
emotional one, the infusion of logic only serves to
confuse the opponent.

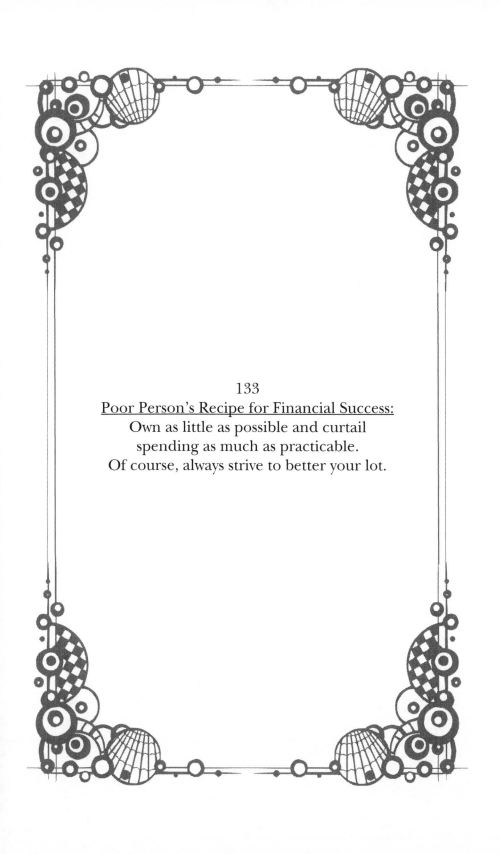

133
<u>Poor Person's Recipe for Financial Success:</u>
Own as little as possible and curtail
spending as much as practicable.
Of course, always strive to better your lot.

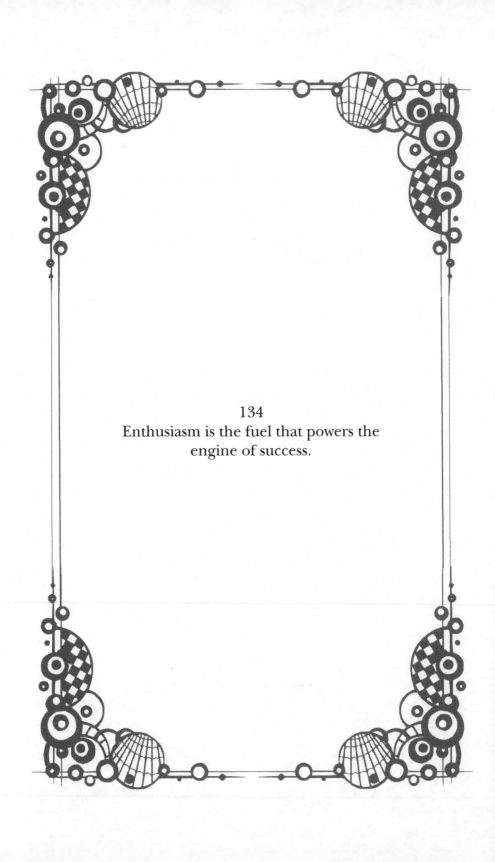

134
Enthusiasm is the fuel that powers the
engine of success.

135
Upon entering a new career at age 57, I re-
formulated a popular Psalms thusly:
"Though I walk through the valley of the shadow of *life*,
I shall fear no evil for thou art with me".

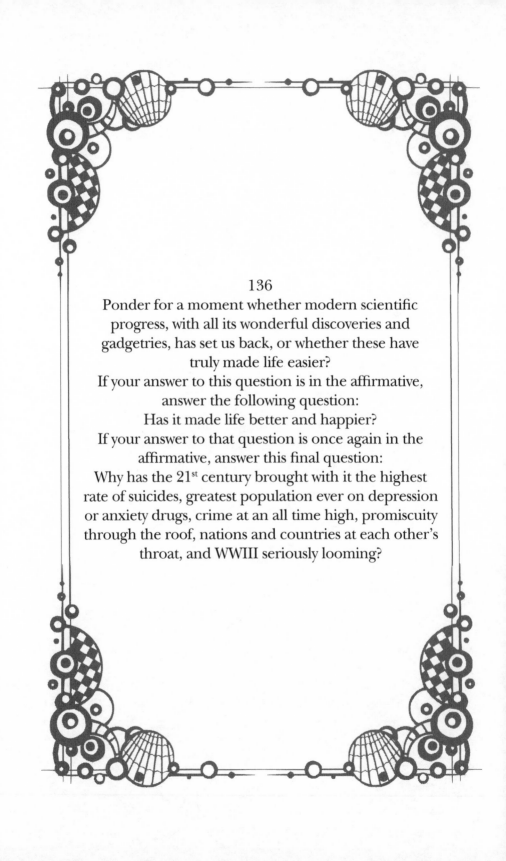

136

Ponder for a moment whether modern scientific progress, with all its wonderful discoveries and gadgetries, has set us back, or whether these have truly made life easier?

If your answer to this question is in the affirmative, answer the following question:

Has it made life better and happier?

If your answer to that question is once again in the affirmative, answer this final question:

Why has the 21st century brought with it the highest rate of suicides, greatest population ever on depression or anxiety drugs, crime at an all time high, promiscuity through the roof, nations and countries at each other's throat, and WWIII seriously looming?

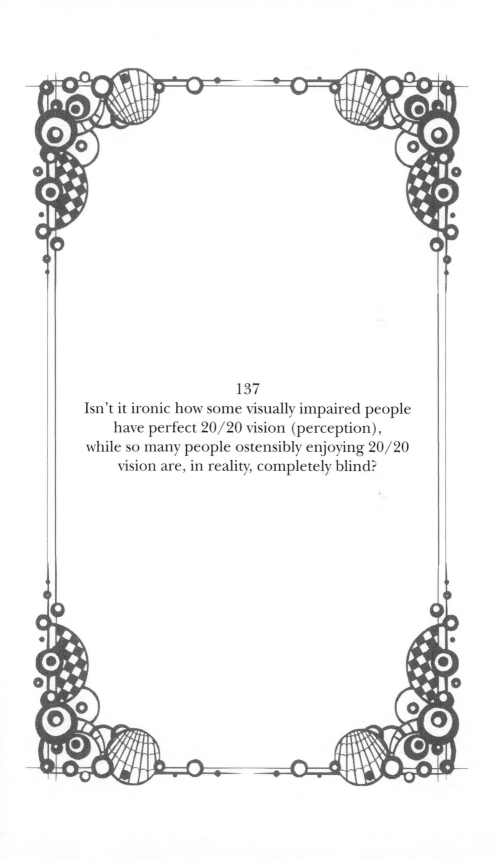

137
Isn't it ironic how some visually impaired people
have perfect 20/20 vision (perception),
while so many people ostensibly enjoying 20/20
vision are, in reality, completely blind?

138
For optimal satisfaction, strive to establish a lifestyle
in accordance with your financial stratum.

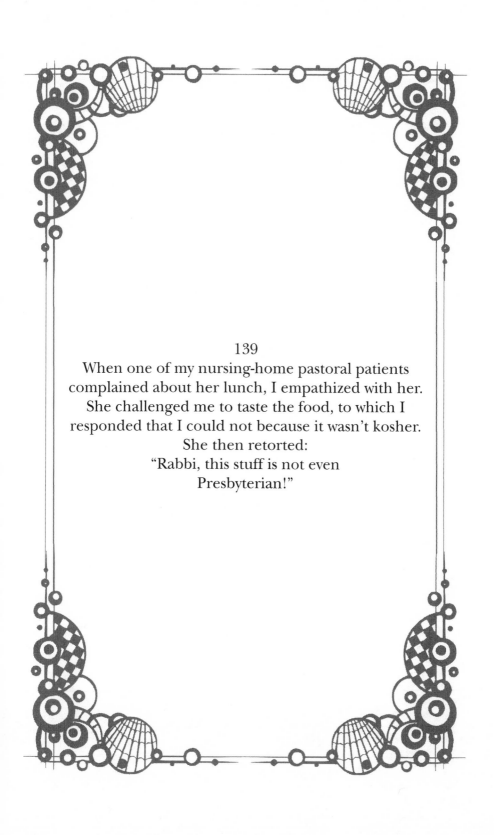

139
When one of my nursing-home pastoral patients
complained about her lunch, I empathized with her.
She challenged me to taste the food, to which I
responded that I could not because it wasn't kosher.
She then retorted:
"Rabbi, this stuff is not even
Presbyterian!"

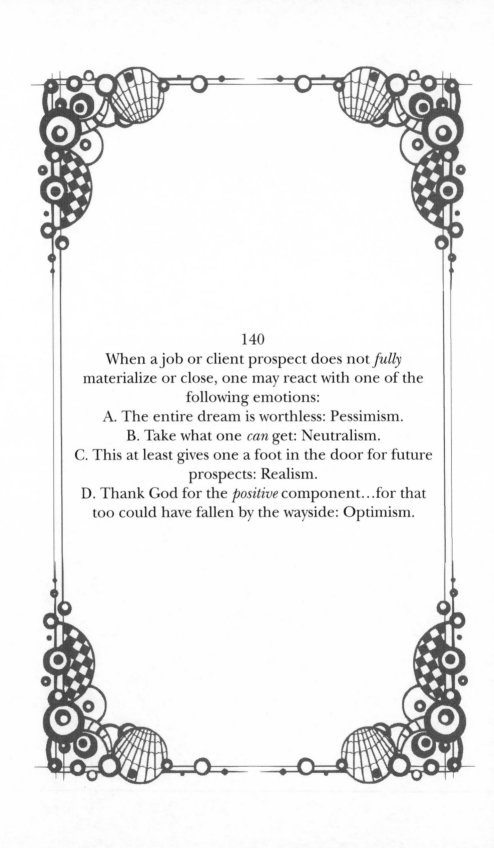

140

When a job or client prospect does not *fully* materialize or close, one may react with one of the following emotions:

A. The entire dream is worthless: Pessimism.

B. Take what one *can* get: Neutralism.

C. This at least gives one a foot in the door for future prospects: Realism.

D. Thank God for the *positive* component...for that too could have fallen by the wayside: Optimism.

141
When *privilege* is accompanied by *responsibility*,
the crown of *respect* is bestowed.

142
In my many years of counseling,
I've heard oh too many times:
I would love to, but she is just too difficult to love.
Isn't that statement oxy moronic?

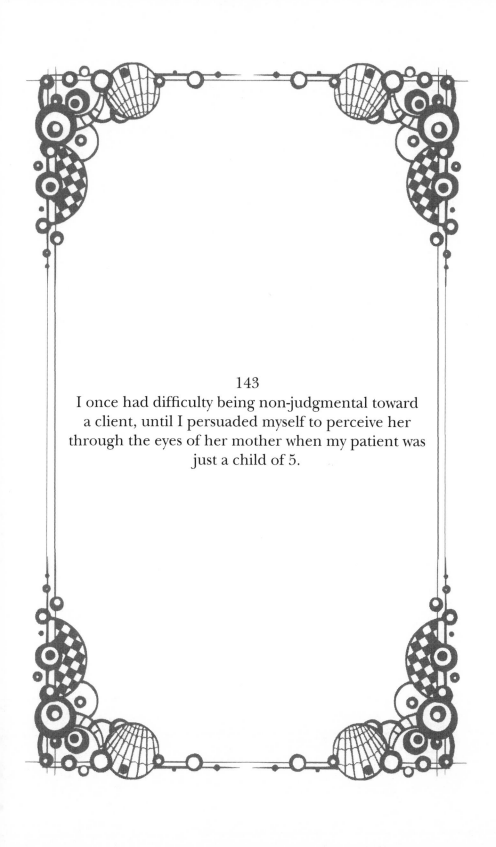

143
I once had difficulty being non-judgmental toward
a client, until I persuaded myself to perceive her
through the eyes of her mother when my patient was
just a child of 5.

144
Through improving our communication skills,
we can learn to live together even in the face of
disagreement and diversity.

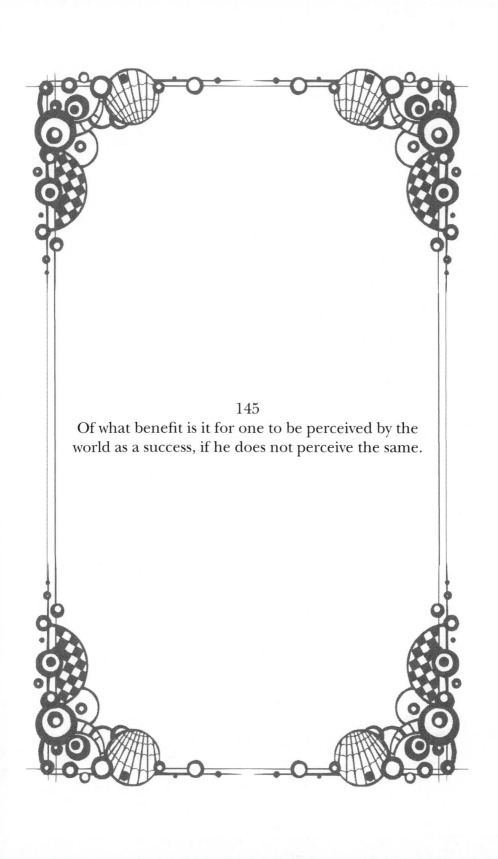

145
Of what benefit is it for one to be perceived by the
world as a success, if he does not perceive the same.

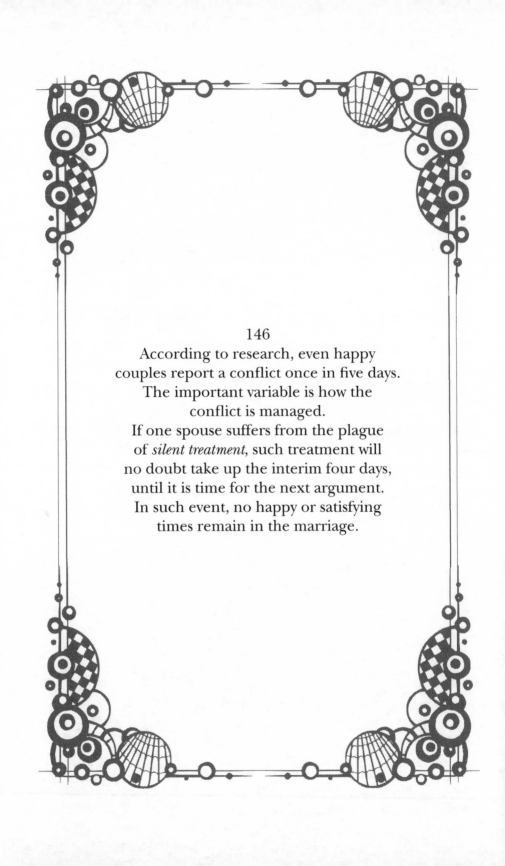

146

According to research, even happy
couples report a conflict once in five days.
The important variable is how the
conflict is managed.
If one spouse suffers from the plague
of *silent treatment,* such treatment will
no doubt take up the interim four days,
until it is time for the next argument.
In such event, no happy or satisfying
times remain in the marriage.

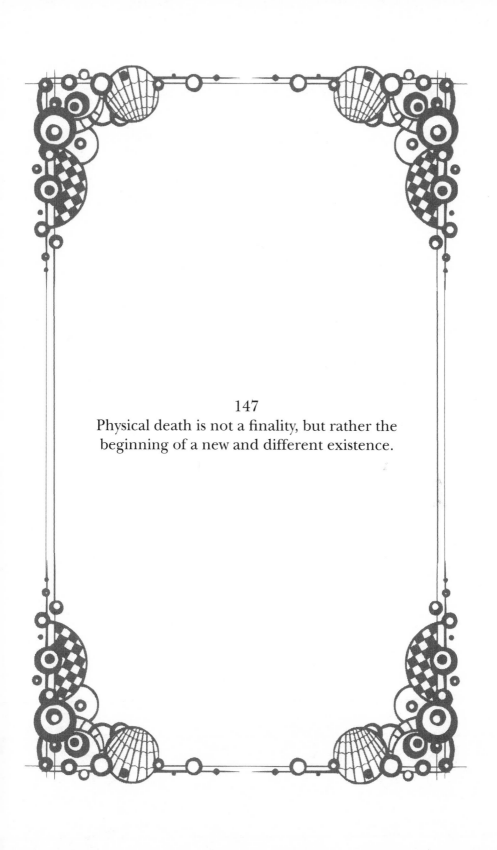

147
Physical death is not a finality, but rather the beginning of a new and different existence.

148
At times, one's perception represents more one's wishful thinking than it does reality.

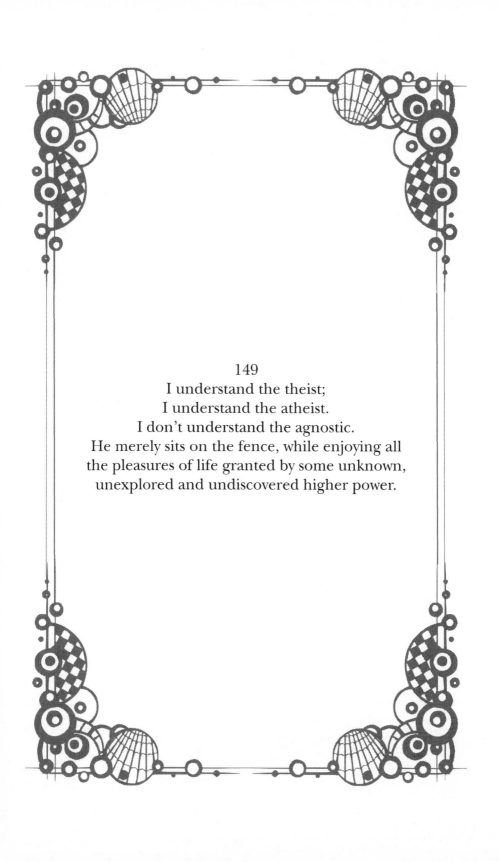

149
I understand the theist;
I understand the atheist.
I don't understand the agnostic.
He merely sits on the fence, while enjoying all
the pleasures of life granted by some unknown,
unexplored and undiscovered higher power.

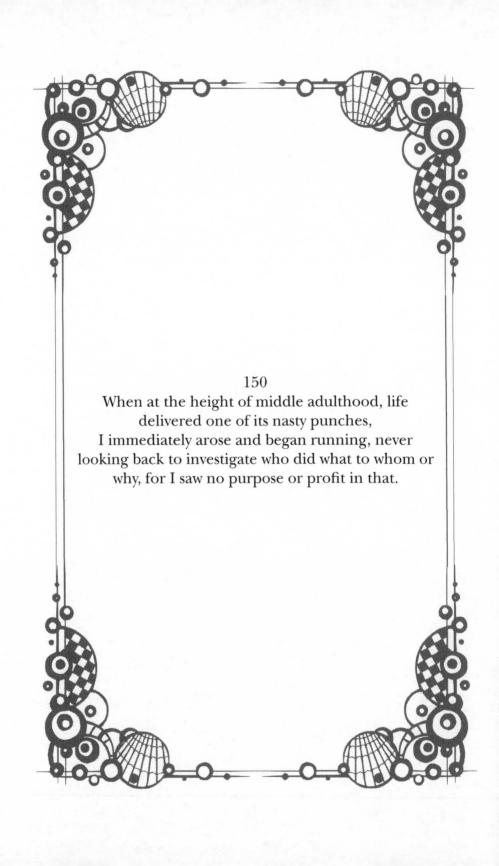

150

When at the height of middle adulthood, life
delivered one of its nasty punches,
I immediately arose and began running, never
looking back to investigate who did what to whom or
why, for I saw no purpose or profit in that.

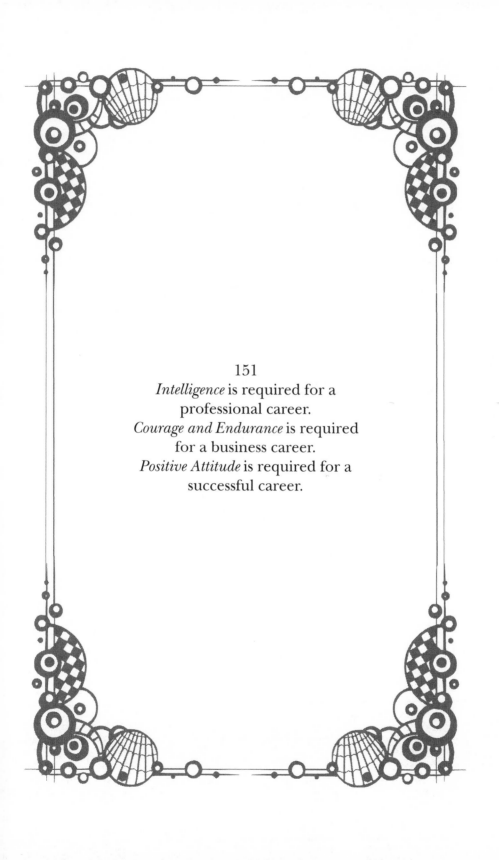

151
Intelligence is required for a
professional career.
Courage and Endurance is required
for a business career.
Positive Attitude is required for a
successful career.

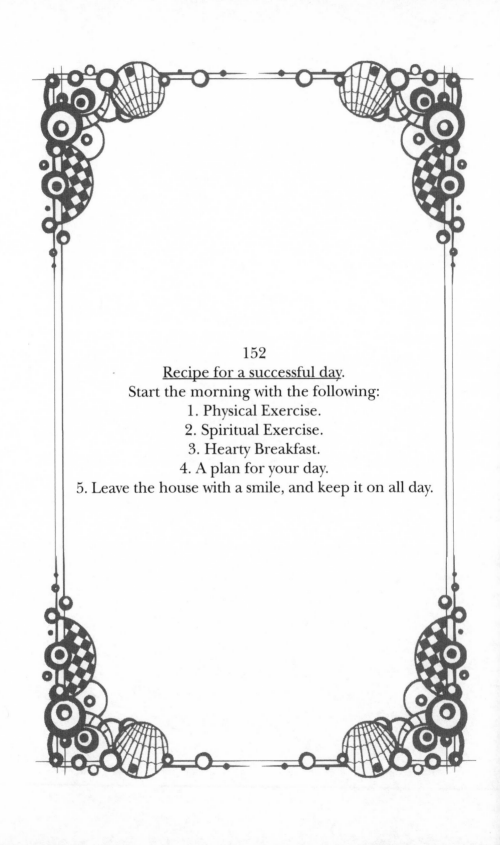

152
<u>Recipe for a successful day</u>.
Start the morning with the following:
1. Physical Exercise.
2. Spiritual Exercise.
3. Hearty Breakfast.
4. A plan for your day.
5. Leave the house with a smile, and keep it on all day.

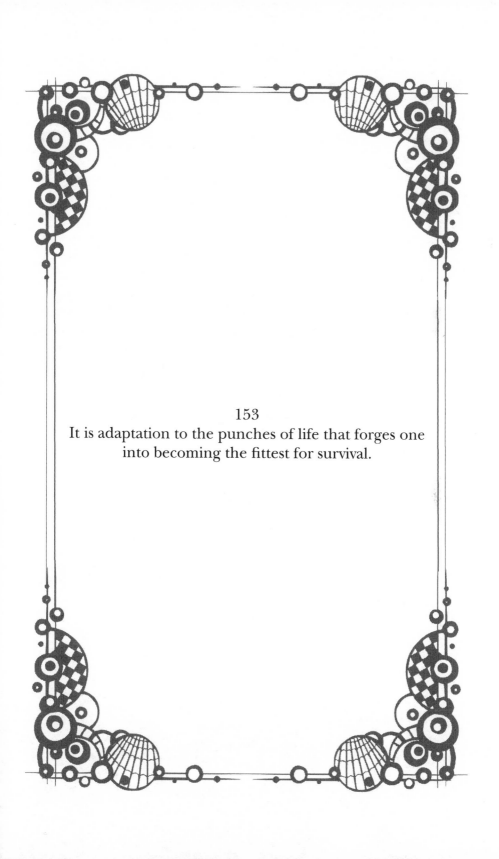

153

It is adaptation to the punches of life that forges one
into becoming the fittest for survival.

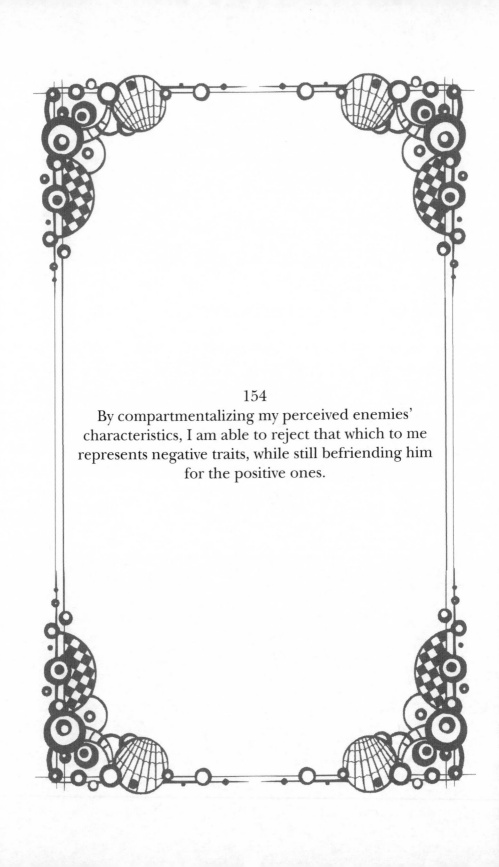

154
By compartmentalizing my perceived enemies'
characteristics, I am able to reject that which to me
represents negative traits, while still befriending him
for the positive ones.

155
A good marriage is where spouses do
not turn into spices.
A spousal marriage is special;
A spicy marriage is a spectacle.

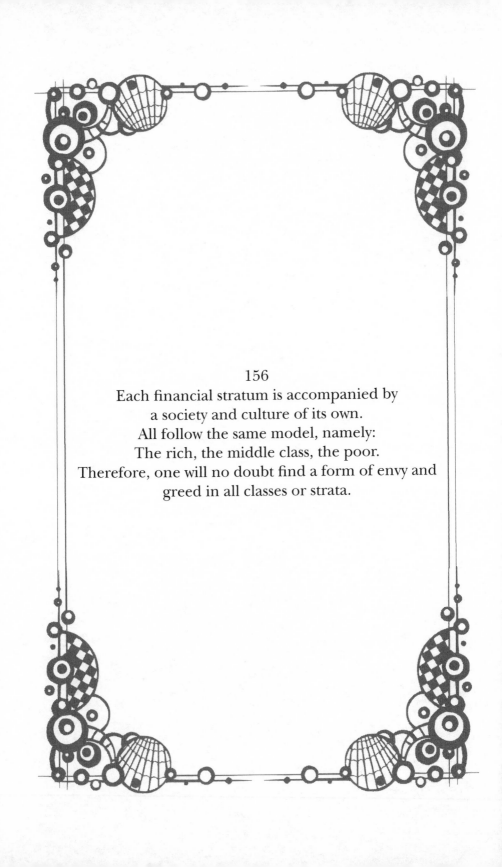

156

Each financial stratum is accompanied by
a society and culture of its own.
All follow the same model, namely:
The rich, the middle class, the poor.
Therefore, one will no doubt find a form of envy and
greed in all classes or strata.

157
Extremism develops into fanaticism,
which in turn devolves into militancy.
The rest is the history of war.

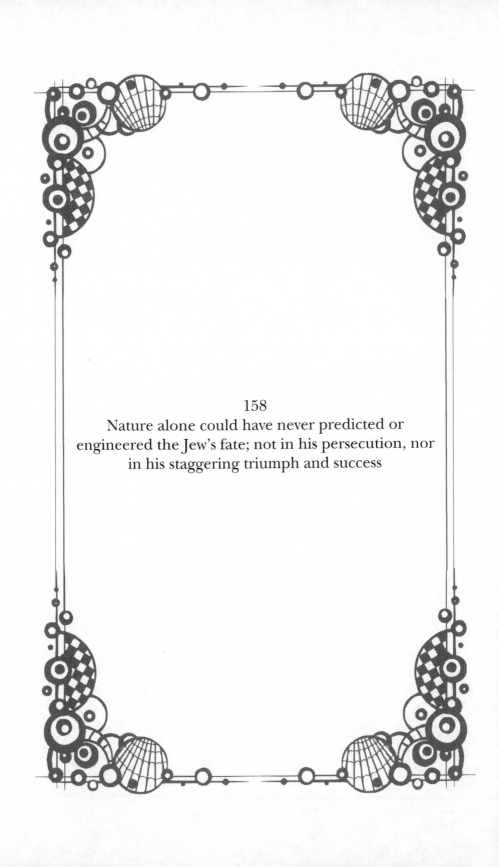

158

Nature alone could have never predicted or
engineered the Jew's fate; not in his persecution, nor
in his staggering triumph and success

159
Rather than awarding material possessions to your
offspring, furnish them with the tools to obtain them
on their own.

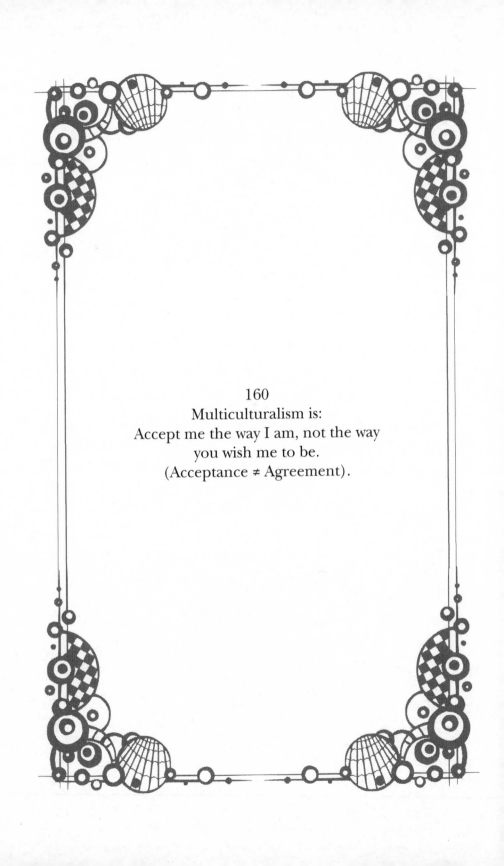

160
Multiculturalism is:
Accept me the way I am, not the way
you wish me to be.
(Acceptance ≠ Agreement).

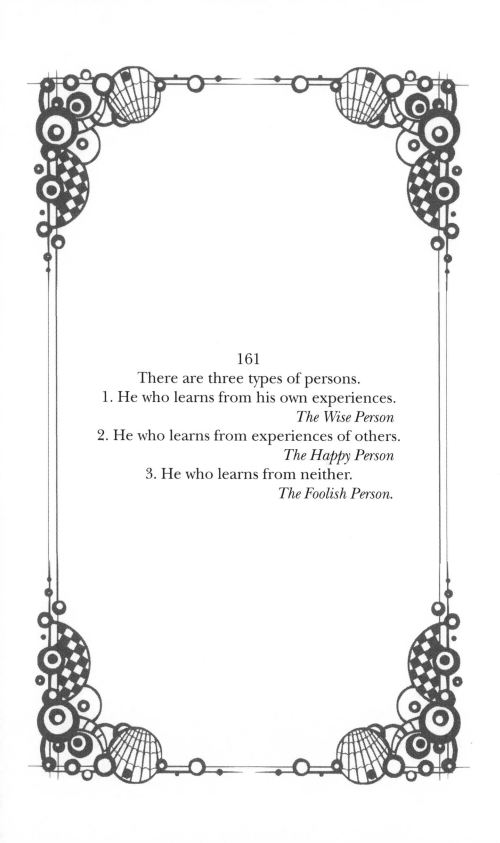

161
There are three types of persons.
1. He who learns from his own experiences.
The Wise Person
2. He who learns from experiences of others.
The Happy Person
3. He who learns from neither.
The Foolish Person.

162
A full handshake is giving of yourself;
A partial handshake is taking for yourself.

163
Getting older is far more palatable than getting old.

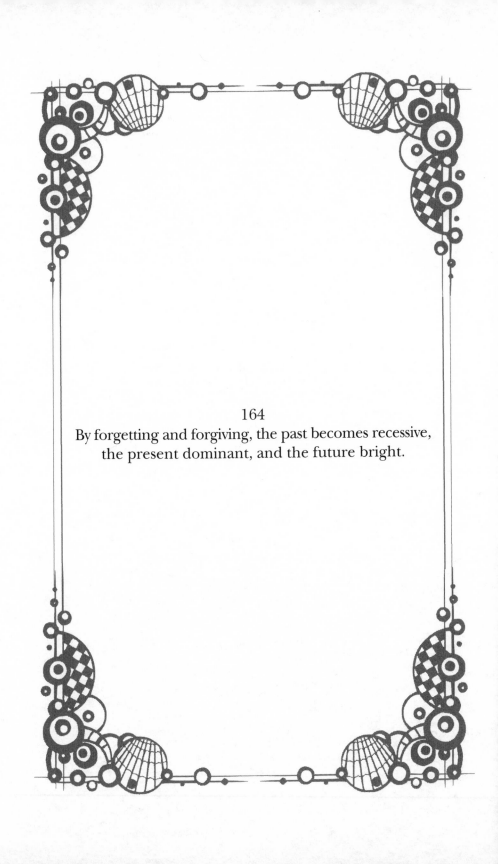

164
By forgetting and forgiving, the past becomes recessive,
the present dominant, and the future bright.

165
When something unfavorable happens to me, I
immediately intellectualize and attempt to find how
things could have turned out worse!

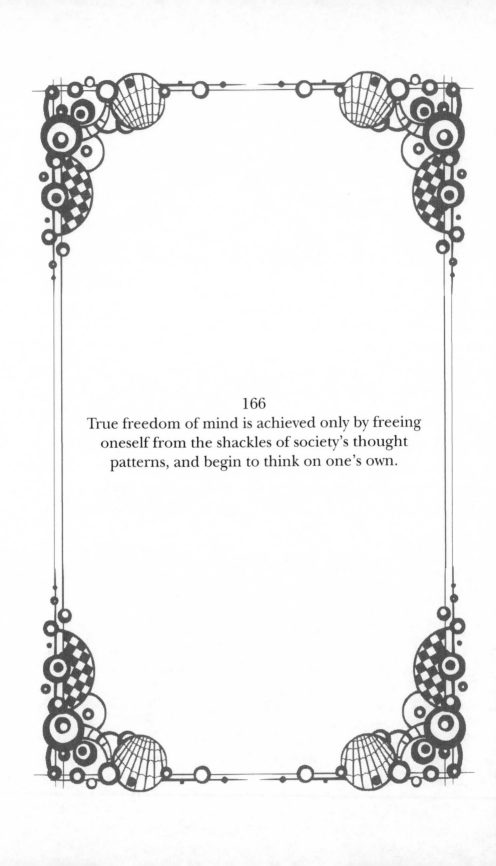

166
True freedom of mind is achieved only by freeing
oneself from the shackles of society's thought
patterns, and begin to think on one's own.

167
Avoidance will surely not resolve the problem.

168
Time is far more precious, and far
more a commodity, than *Money*.
Whereas *Money* may be earned, saved, borrowed,
repaid, and or replenished;
Time may not.

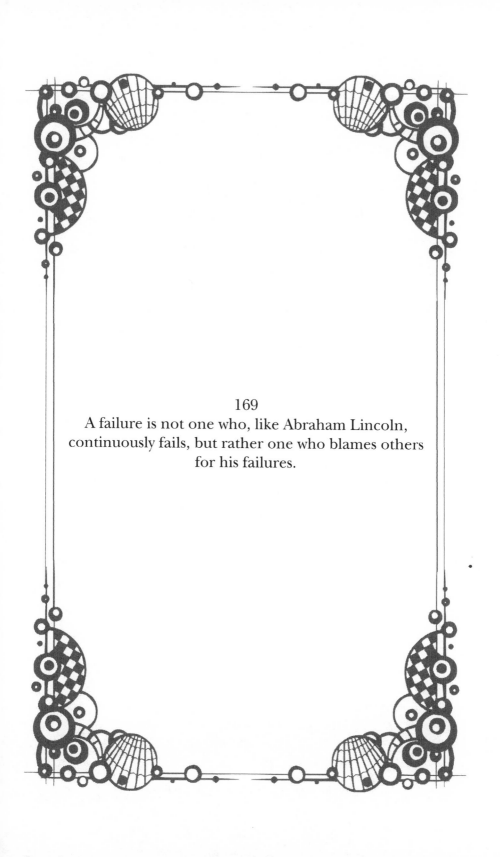

169
A failure is not one who, like Abraham Lincoln,
continuously fails, but rather one who blames others
for his failures.

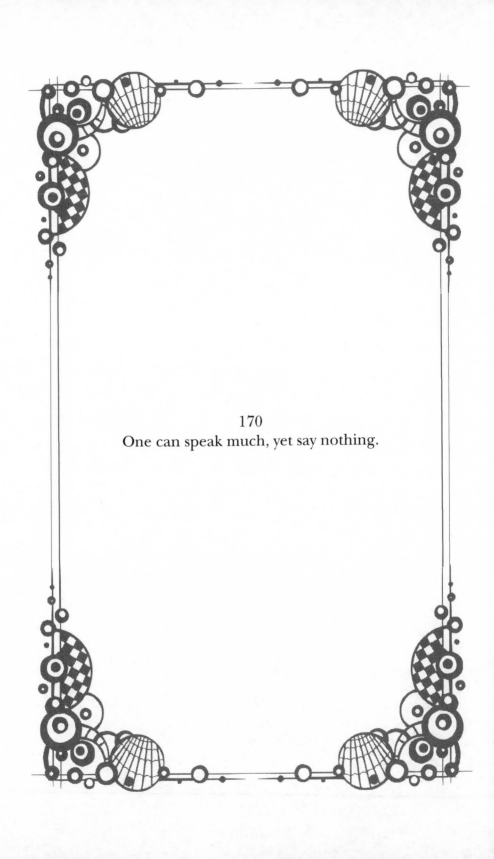

170
One can speak much, yet say nothing.

171
A dream is an attainable goal, whereas a fantasy is
simply that – a fantasy.

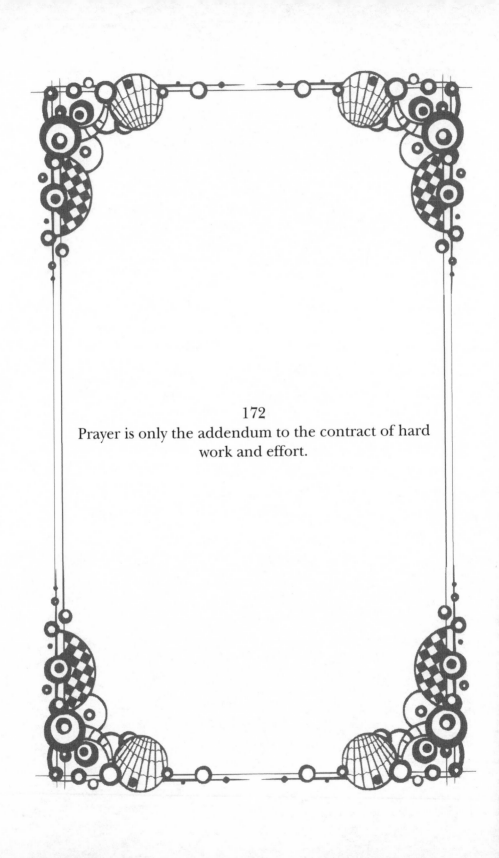

172
Prayer is only the addendum to the contract of hard work and effort.

173
The minute was created for much more than just to
wait.

174
Perfectionism is nothing more than a defense
mechanism to combat the fear of failure, which
emanates from low self-esteem.

175
While taking a substance abuse test at age 59, I
realized that life is filled with tests.

176
If you want to speak *about* me,
I wish you'd speak *to* me.

177
The question is not
Do I have the time?
But rather,
Is it a priority?
If it is, I will find the time.

178
Being happy with your financial lot means
living within your means.

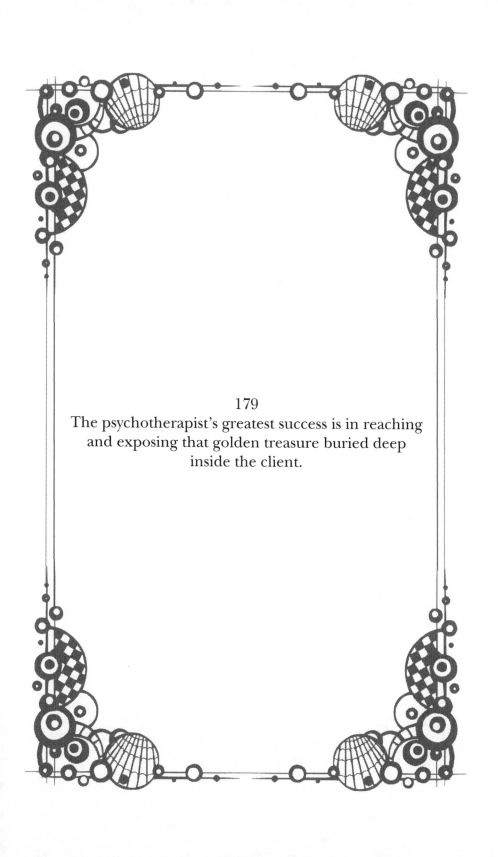

179
The psychotherapist's greatest success is in reaching
and exposing that golden treasure buried deep
inside the client.

180
When one's desire is strong enough to accomplish a
task, his words of choice are not
I will *try*, but rather
I *will*!

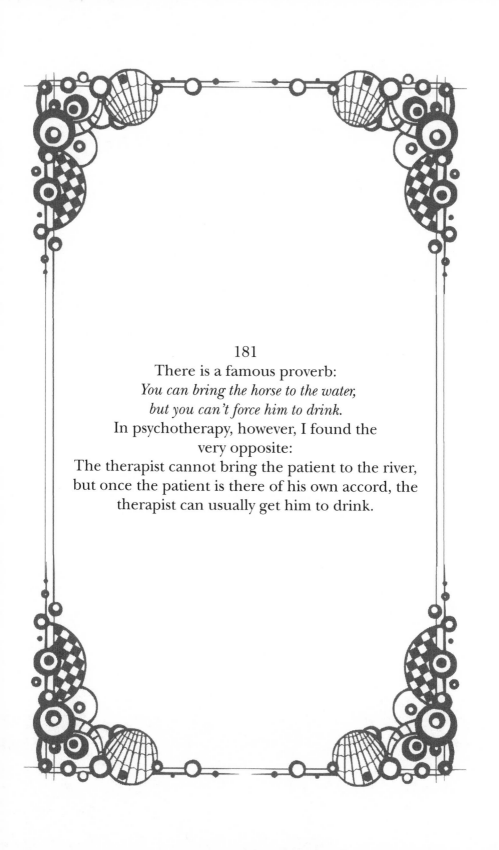

181
There is a famous proverb:
You can bring the horse to the water,
but you can't force him to drink.
In psychotherapy, however, I found the
very opposite:
The therapist cannot bring the patient to the river,
but once the patient is there of his own accord, the
therapist can usually get him to drink.

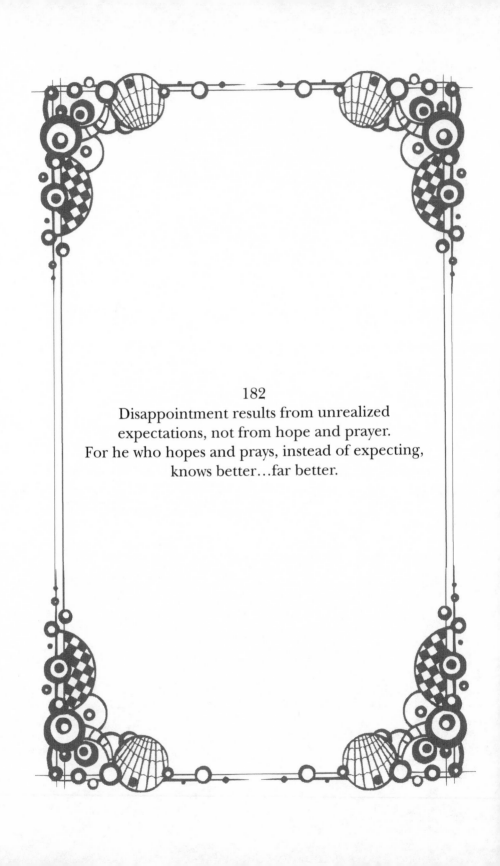

182

Disappointment results from unrealized
expectations, not from hope and prayer.
For he who hopes and prays, instead of expecting,
knows better…far better.

183
It is okay to dream of palaces…
so long as one awakens too.

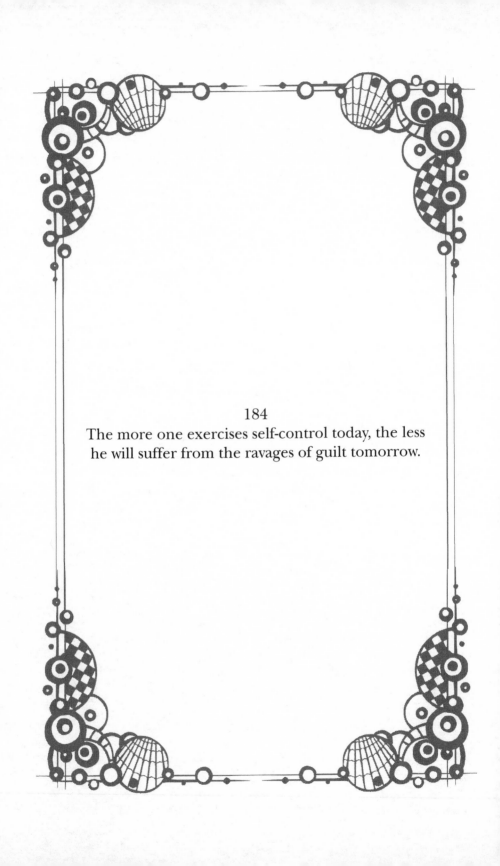

184
The more one exercises self-control today, the less
he will suffer from the ravages of guilt tomorrow.

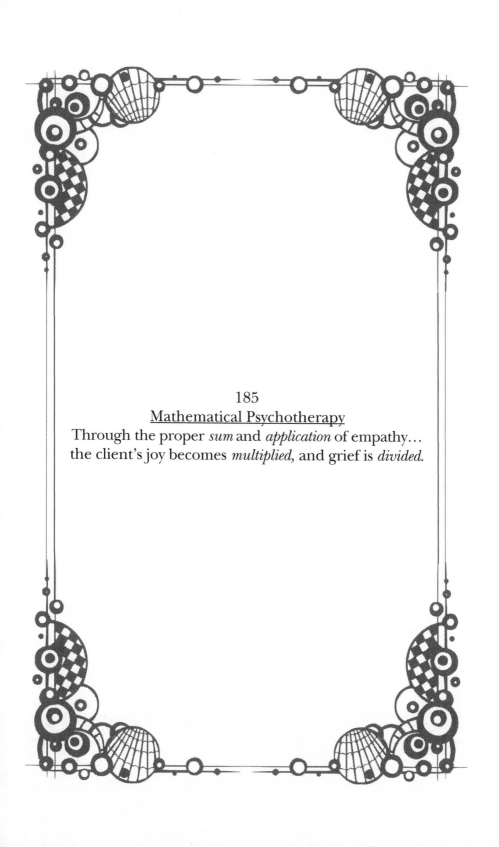

185
<u>Mathematical Psychotherapy</u>
Through the proper *sum* and *application* of empathy…
the client's joy becomes *multiplied,* and grief is *divided.*

186
A client in pain remarked:
A painful day is better than a wasted
one or none at all

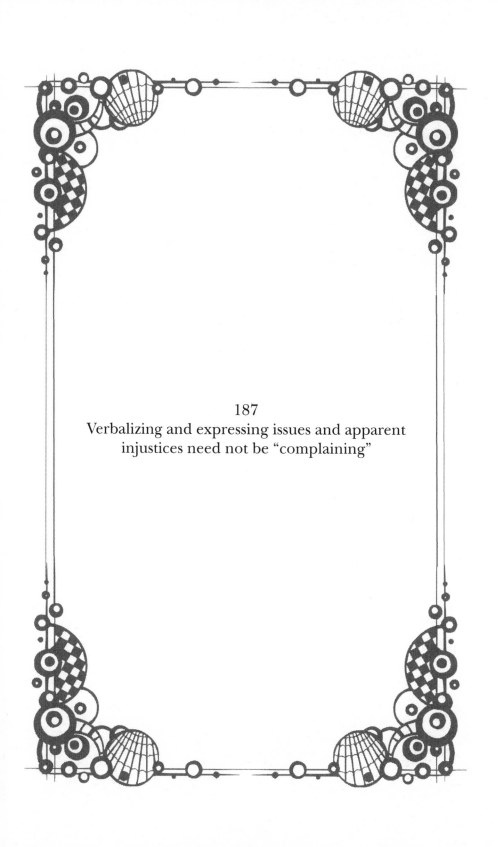

187
Verbalizing and expressing issues and apparent injustices need not be "complaining"

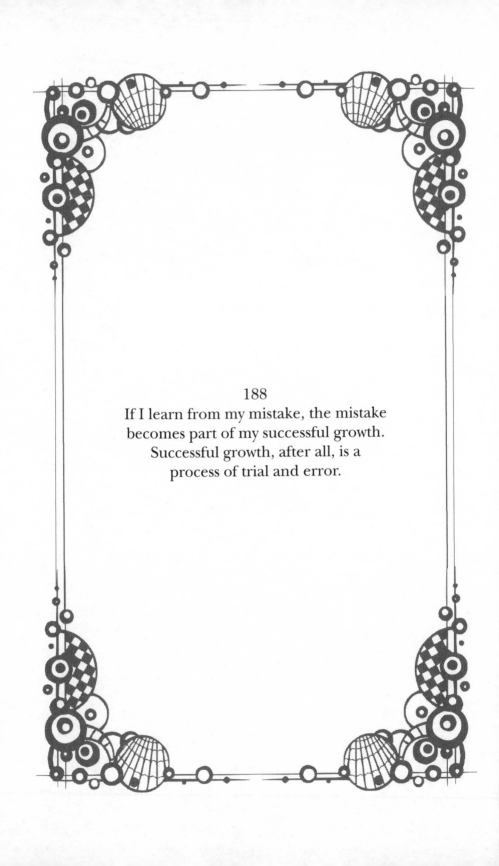

188
If I learn from my mistake, the mistake
becomes part of my successful growth.
Successful growth, after all, is a
process of trial and error.

189
If it's grim today,
it'll likely get brighter tomorrow...
Always Hope!

190
In order to reach life's highs, one must
overcome its lows.

191
Hope is the chicken; optimism the egg.
Don't care which came first.
It also makes no difference.

192
When enslaved to emotion, one's
blurred to intellect.

193
Nothing can be done with the past,
except learn from it.
The tragedy, however, is that we usually don't.

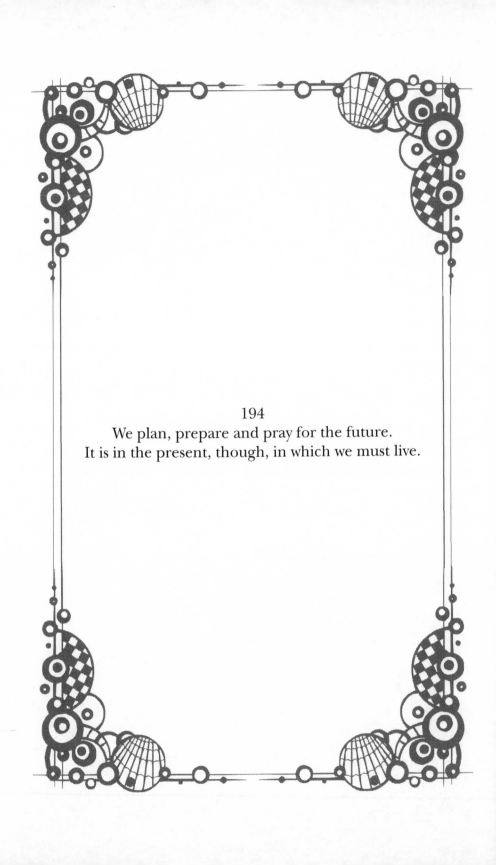

194
We plan, prepare and pray for the future.
It is in the present, though, in which we must live.

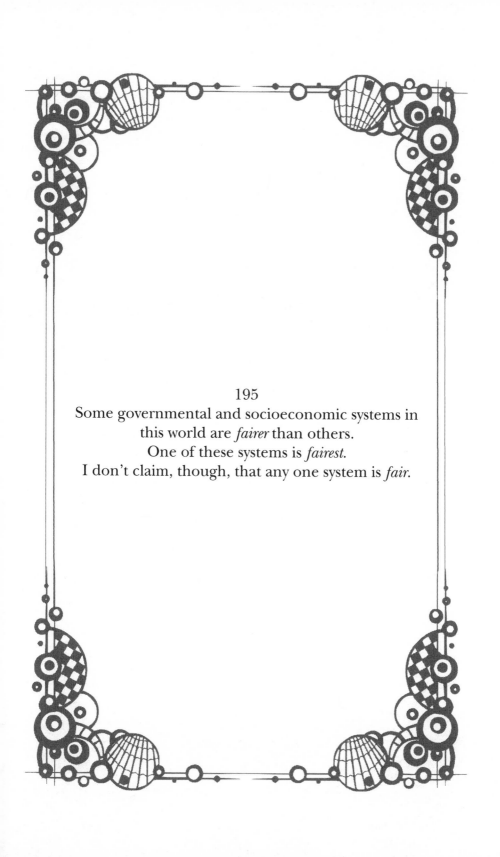

195
Some governmental and socioeconomic systems in
this world are *fairer* than others.
One of these systems is *fairest*.
I don't claim, though, that any one system is *fair*.

196
<u>A Prayer:</u>
Please Lord, grant me the tranquility not only to accept those things I cannot change in life, but in addition, help me get habituated to them, so that I may live with them in the best of health, and with the greatest of joy and happiness.

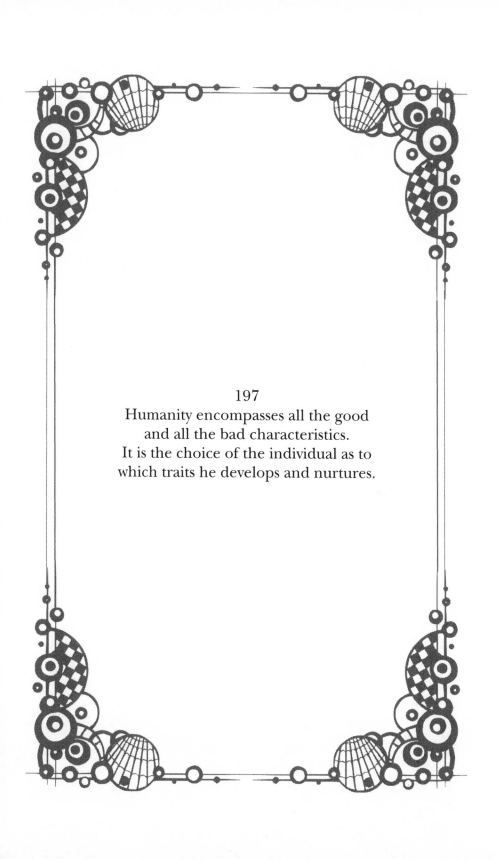

197
Humanity encompasses all the good
and all the bad characteristics.
It is the choice of the individual as to
which traits he develops and nurtures.

198
More important than how others feel about you, is
how you feel about yourself.

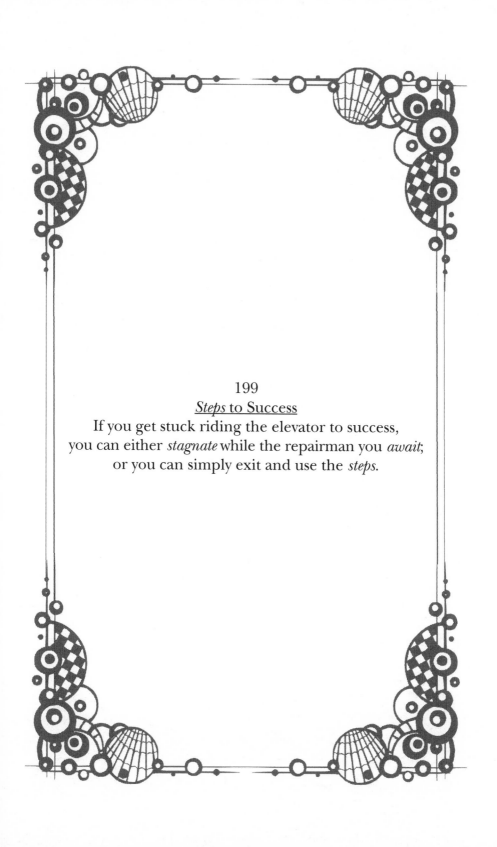

199
Steps to Success
If you get stuck riding the elevator to success,
you can either _stagnate_ while the repairman you _await_,
or you can simply exit and use the _steps_.

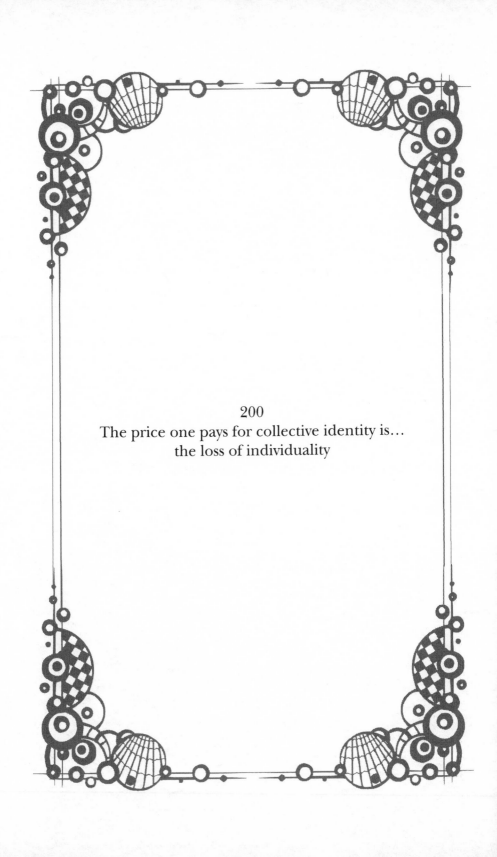

200
The price one pays for collective identity is…
the loss of individuality

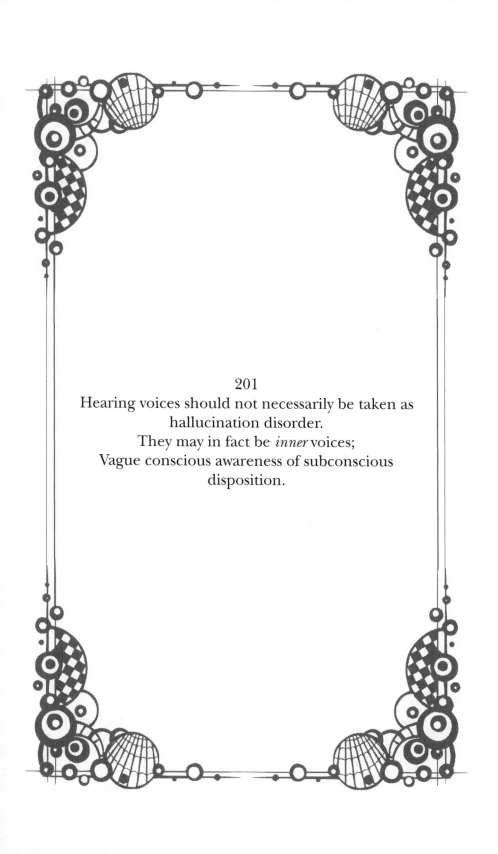

201
Hearing voices should not necessarily be taken as
hallucination disorder.
They may in fact be *inner* voices;
Vague conscious awareness of subconscious
disposition.

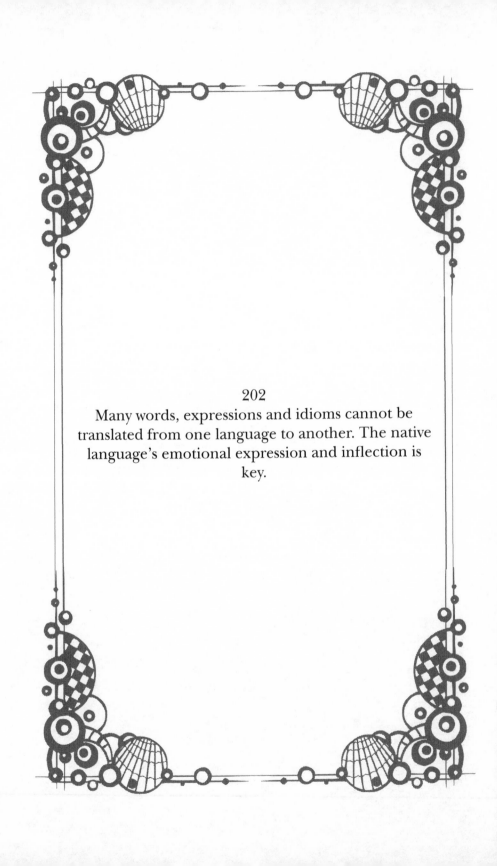

202
Many words, expressions and idioms cannot be translated from one language to another. The native language's emotional expression and inflection is key.

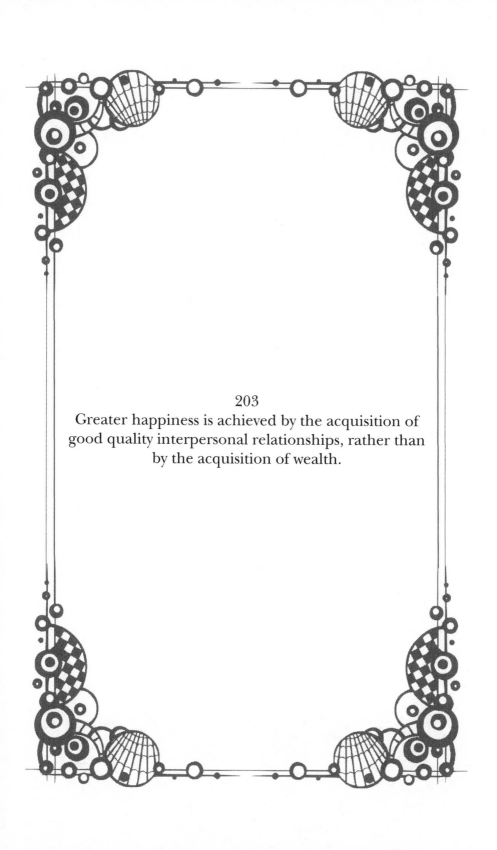

203

Greater happiness is achieved by the acquisition of good quality interpersonal relationships, rather than by the acquisition of wealth.

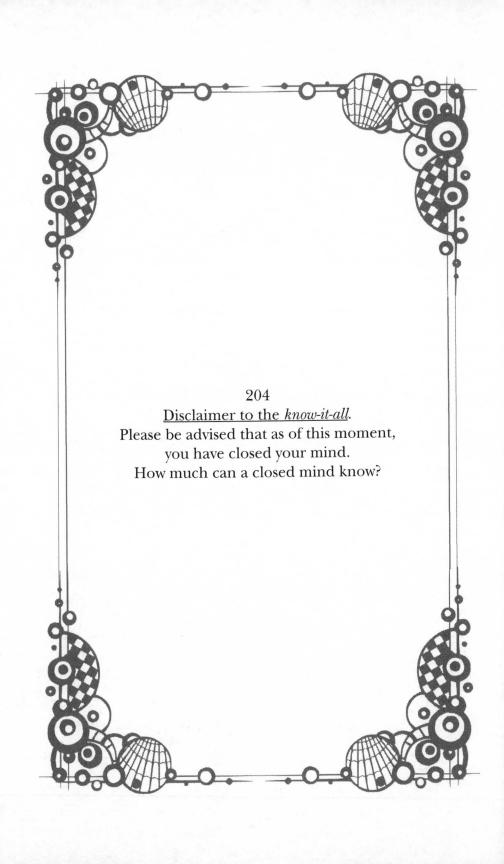

204
<u>Disclaimer to the *know-it-all*.</u>
Please be advised that as of this moment,
you have closed your mind.
How much can a closed mind know?

205
The universal and ultimate silver lining can be found
in the words of King David:
*"Everything that happens does so because it fits into the
Greater Divine scheme of the universe, and is
therefore good"*.
(Psalms, 145:9)

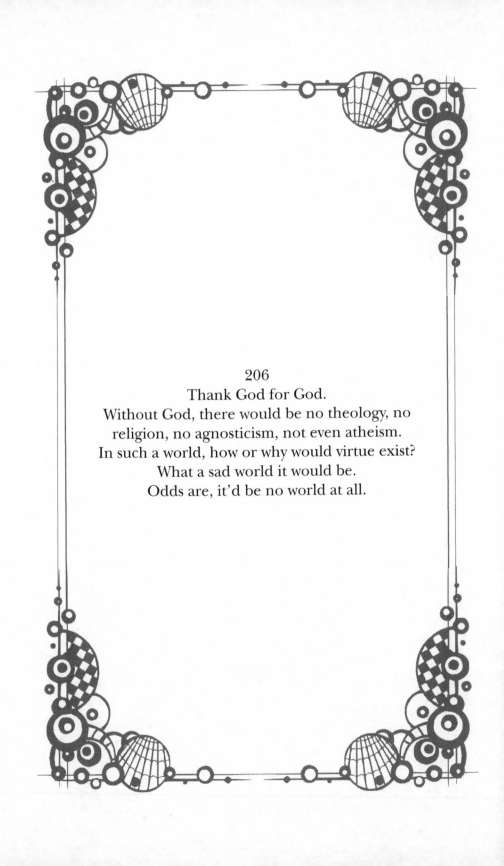

206
Thank God for God.
Without God, there would be no theology, no
religion, no agnosticism, not even atheism.
In such a world, how or why would virtue exist?
What a sad world it would be.
Odds are, it'd be no world at all.

207
The more you bear, the more you learn
how to bear more.

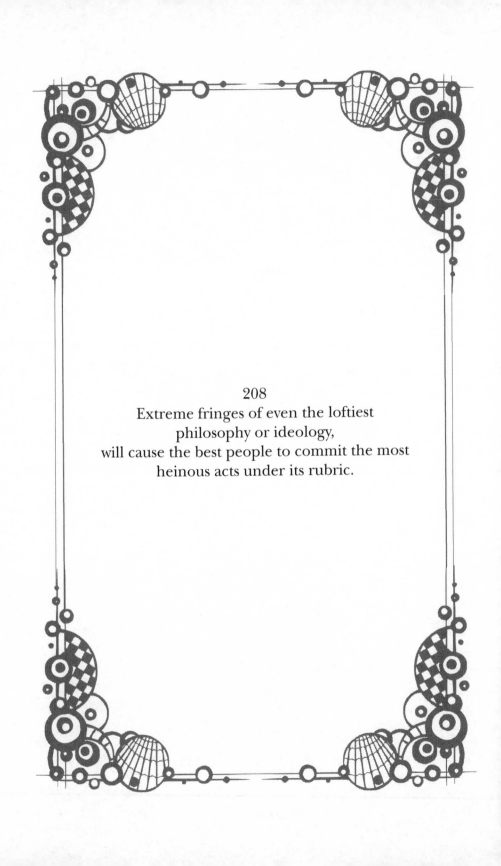

208
Extreme fringes of even the loftiest
philosophy or ideology,
will cause the best people to commit the most
heinous acts under its rubric.

209
Wealth is like a scalpel;
one wrong move, and…

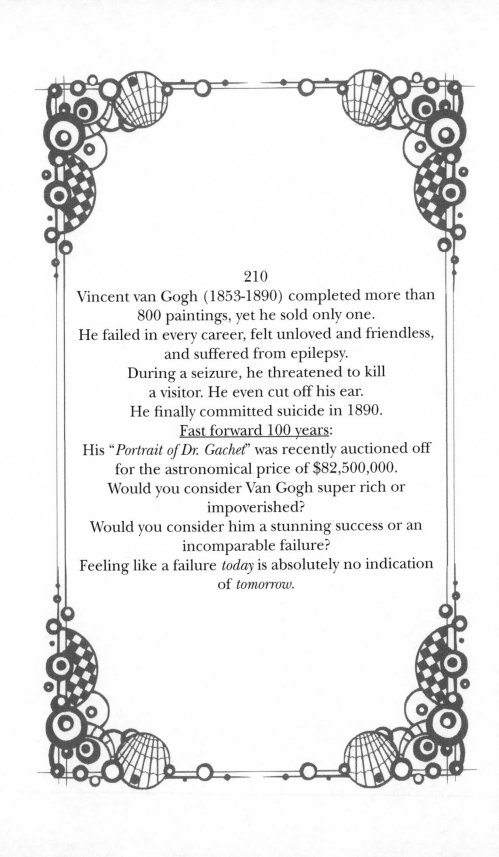

210

Vincent van Gogh (1853-1890) completed more than 800 paintings, yet he sold only one.

He failed in every career, felt unloved and friendless, and suffered from epilepsy.

During a seizure, he threatened to kill a visitor. He even cut off his ear.

He finally committed suicide in 1890.

<u>Fast forward 100 years</u>:

His *"Portrait of Dr. Gachet"* was recently auctioned off for the astronomical price of $82,500,000.

Would you consider Van Gogh super rich or impoverished?

Would you consider him a stunning success or an incomparable failure?

Feeling like a failure *today* is absolutely no indication of *tomorrow.*

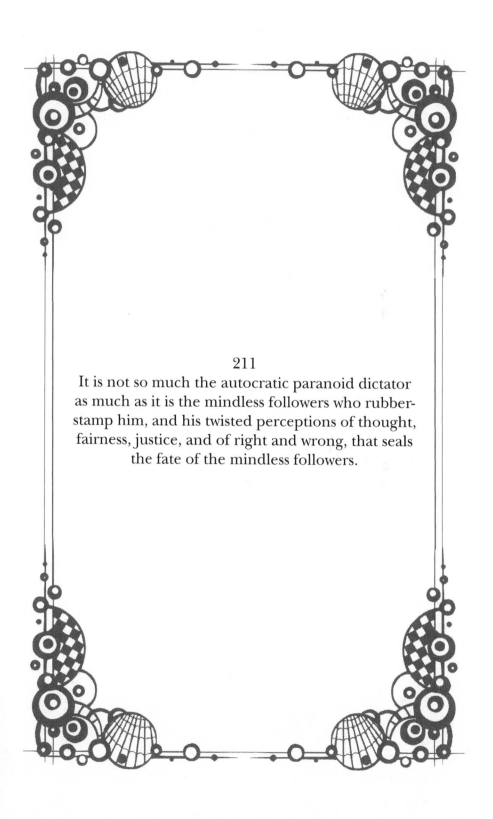

211
It is not so much the autocratic paranoid dictator as much as it is the mindless followers who rubber-stamp him, and his twisted perceptions of thought, fairness, justice, and of right and wrong, that seals the fate of the mindless followers.

212
It is far better to achieve 50% of high goals,
than 100% of low ones.

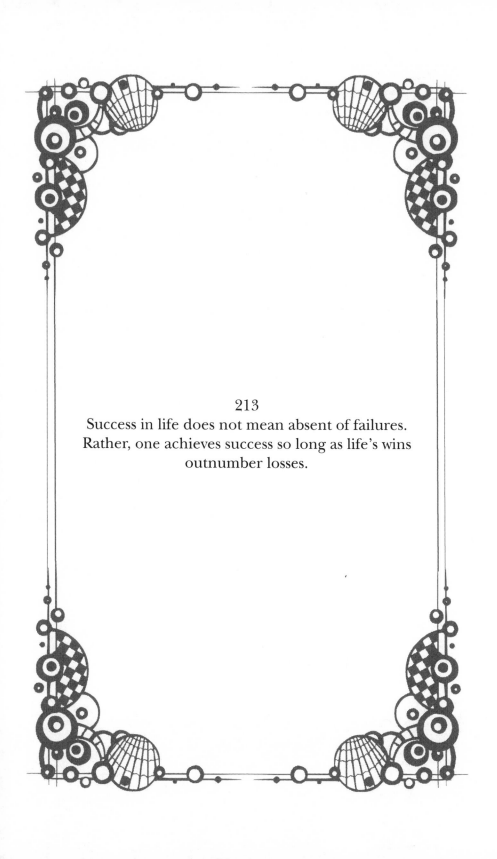

213
Success in life does not mean absent of failures.
Rather, one achieves success so long as life's wins
outnumber losses.

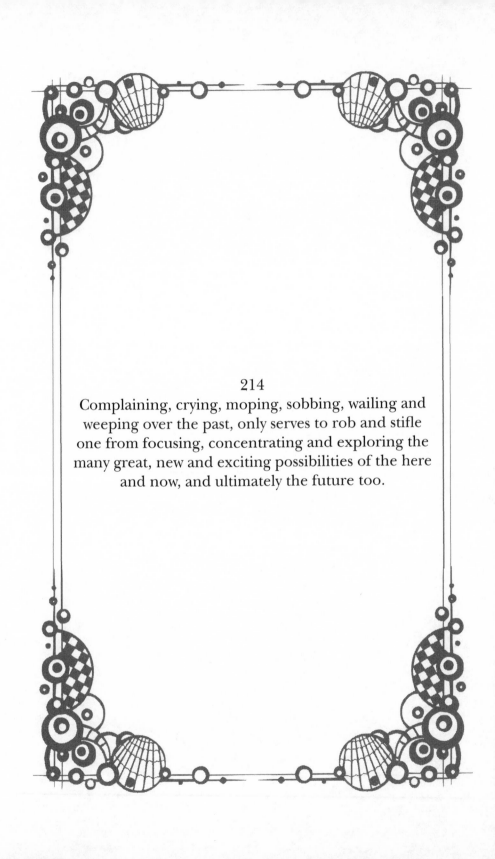

214

Complaining, crying, moping, sobbing, wailing and weeping over the past, only serves to rob and stifle one from focusing, concentrating and exploring the many great, new and exciting possibilities of the here and now, and ultimately the future too.

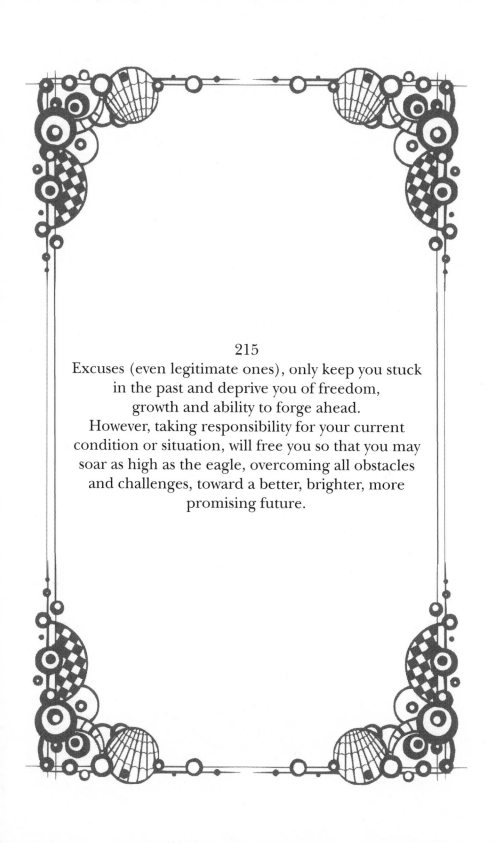

215

Excuses (even legitimate ones), only keep you stuck
in the past and deprive you of freedom,
growth and ability to forge ahead.
However, taking responsibility for your current
condition or situation, will free you so that you may
soar as high as the eagle, overcoming all obstacles
and challenges, toward a better, brighter, more
promising future.

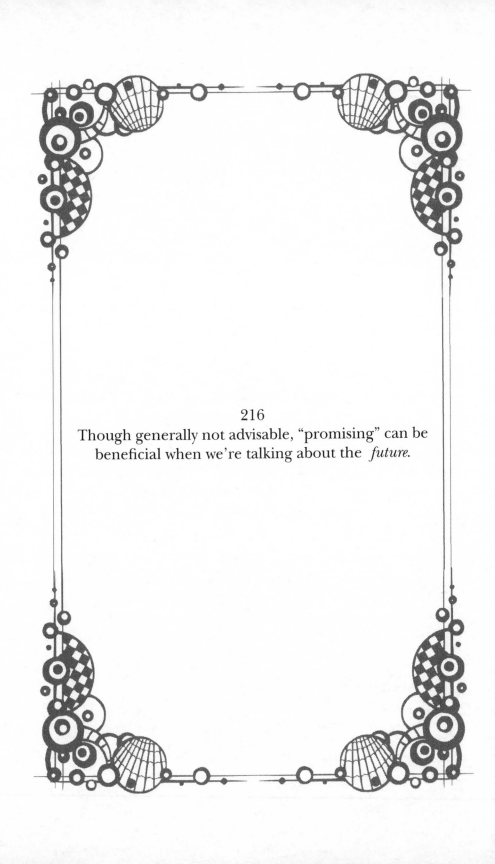

216
Though generally not advisable, "promising" can be beneficial when we're talking about the *future*.

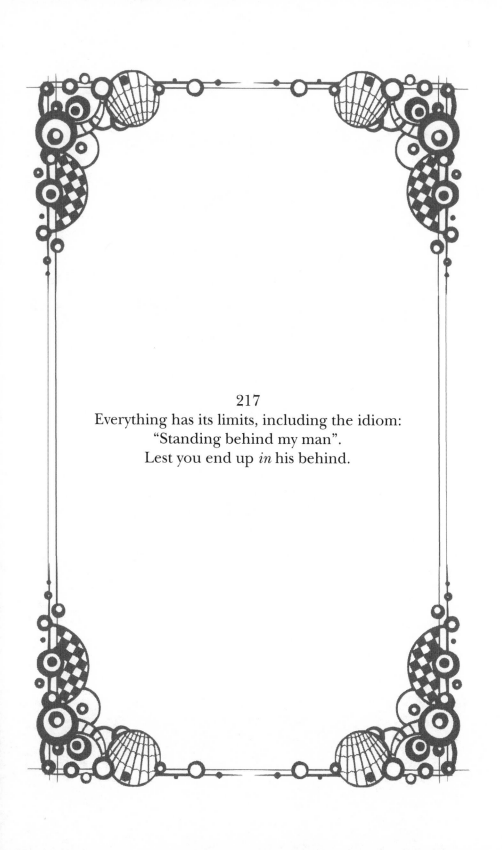

217
Everything has its limits, including the idiom:
"Standing behind my man".
Lest you end up *in* his behind.

218
Strength lies not in numbers, but rather in its unity.

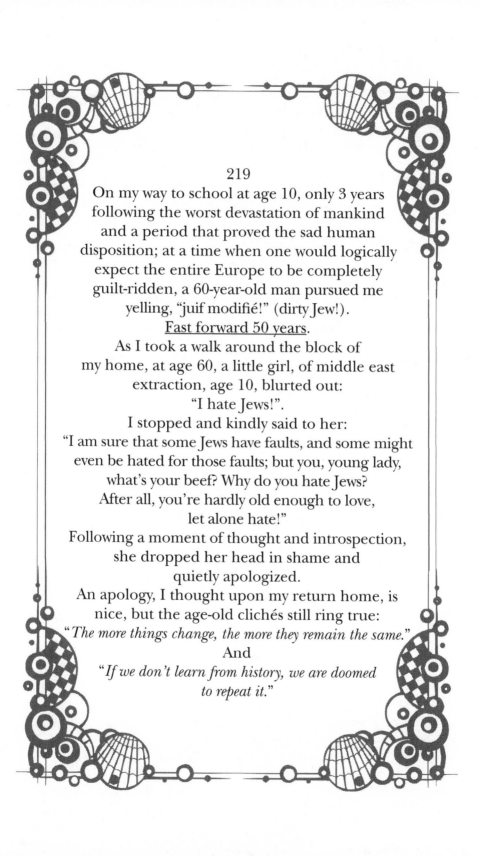

219

On my way to school at age 10, only 3 years
following the worst devastation of mankind
and a period that proved the sad human
disposition; at a time when one would logically
expect the entire Europe to be completely
guilt-ridden, a 60-year-old man pursued me
yelling, "juif modifié!" (dirty Jew!).
<u>Fast forward 50 years</u>.
As I took a walk around the block of
my home, at age 60, a little girl, of middle east
extraction, age 10, blurted out:
"I hate Jews!".
I stopped and kindly said to her:
"I am sure that some Jews have faults, and some might
even be hated for those faults; but you, young lady,
what's your beef? Why do you hate Jews?
After all, you're hardly old enough to love,
let alone hate!"
Following a moment of thought and introspection,
she dropped her head in shame and
quietly apologized.
An apology, I thought upon my return home, is
nice, but the age-old clichés still ring true:
"The more things change, the more they remain the same."
And
*"If we don't learn from history, we are doomed
to repeat it."*

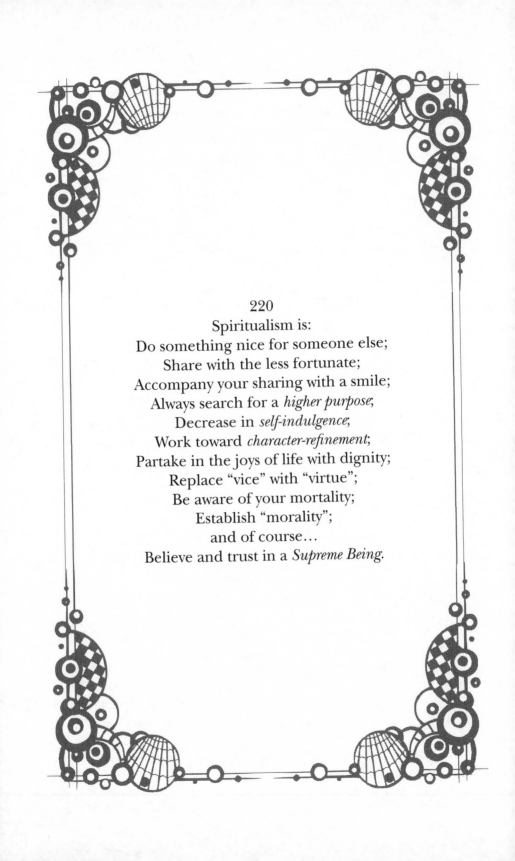

220
Spiritualism is:
Do something nice for someone else;
Share with the less fortunate;
Accompany your sharing with a smile;
Always search for a *higher purpose*;
Decrease in *self-indulgence*;
Work toward *character-refinement*;
Partake in the joys of life with dignity;
Replace "vice" with "virtue";
Be aware of your mortality;
Establish "morality";
and of course…
Believe and trust in a *Supreme Being*.

221
If you have no purpose in life,
you have no reason to live.

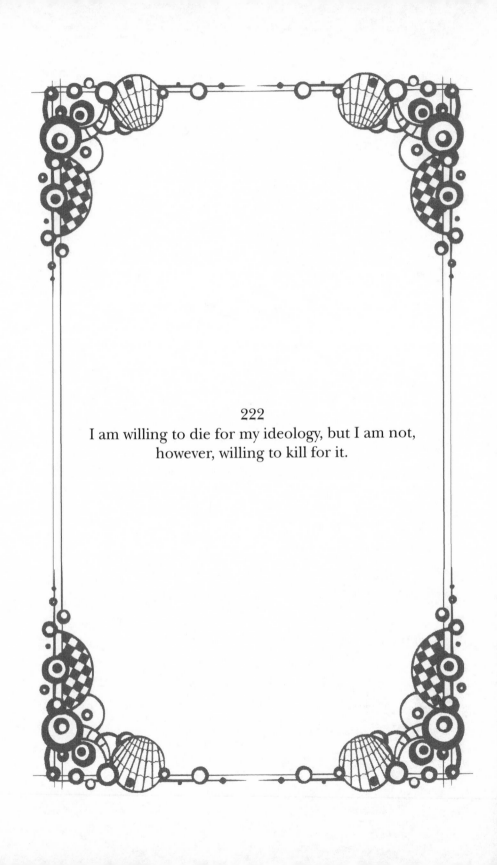

222

I am willing to die for my ideology, but I am not, however, willing to kill for it.

223
In a relationship with no
communication, the slightest match-
spark quickly erupts into a full-blown volcano.
How many volcanoes can one relationship endure?

224
Along with success comes the ability
to accept failures.

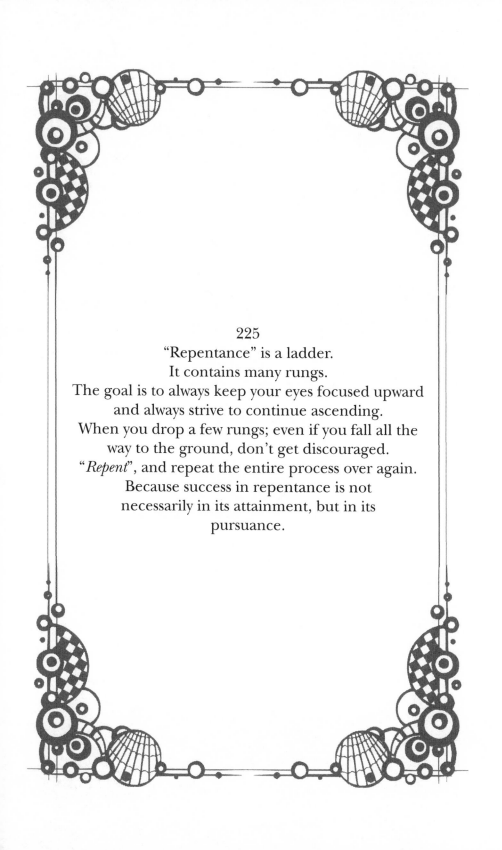

225

"Repentance" is a ladder.

It contains many rungs.

The goal is to always keep your eyes focused upward and always strive to continue ascending.

When you drop a few rungs; even if you fall all the way to the ground, don't get discouraged.

"*Repent*", and repeat the entire process over again.

Because success in repentance is not necessarily in its attainment, but in its pursuance.

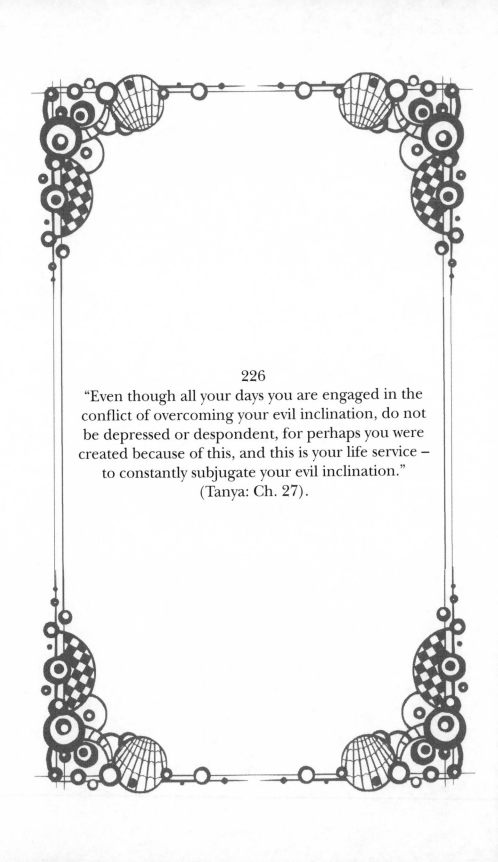

226

"Even though all your days you are engaged in the conflict of overcoming your evil inclination, do not be depressed or despondent, for perhaps you were created because of this, and this is your life service – to constantly subjugate your evil inclination."
(Tanya: Ch. 27).

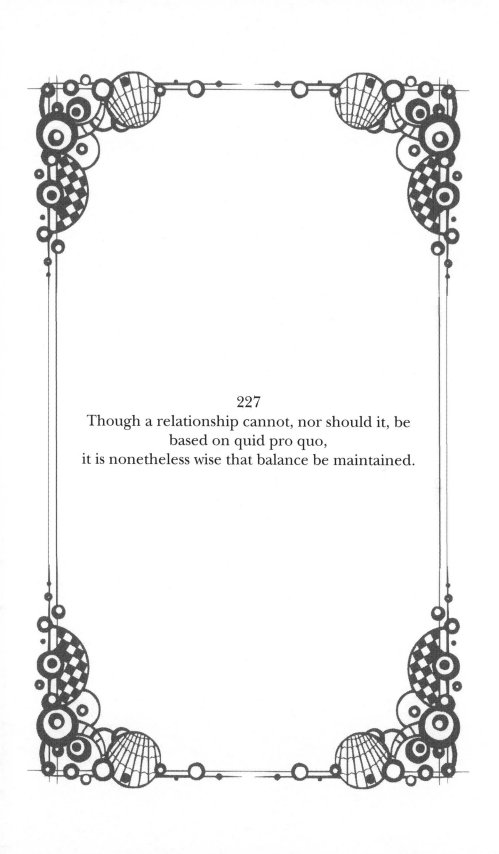

227
Though a relationship cannot, nor should it, be
based on quid pro quo,
it is nonetheless wise that balance be maintained.

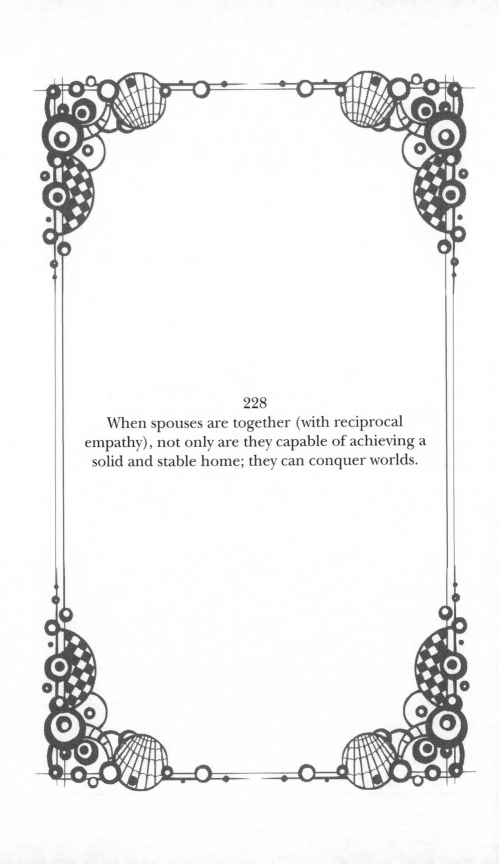

228
When spouses are together (with reciprocal empathy), not only are they capable of achieving a solid and stable home; they can conquer worlds.

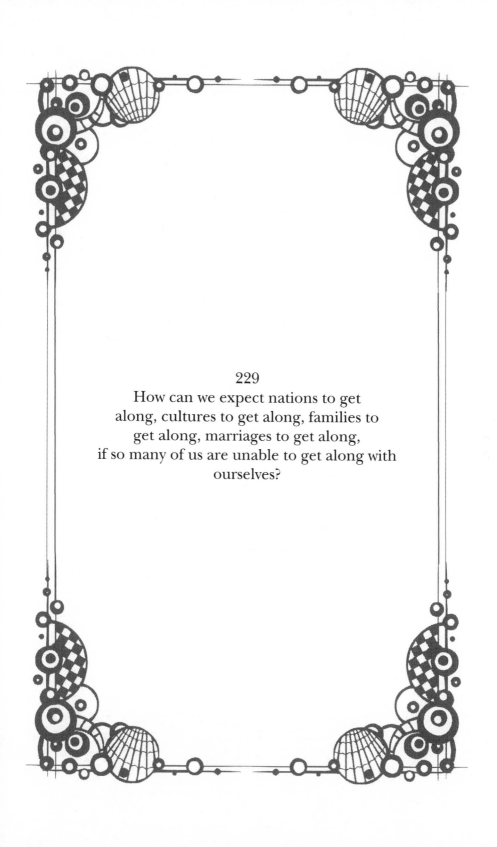

229
How can we expect nations to get
along, cultures to get along, families to
get along, marriages to get along,
if so many of us are unable to get along with
ourselves?

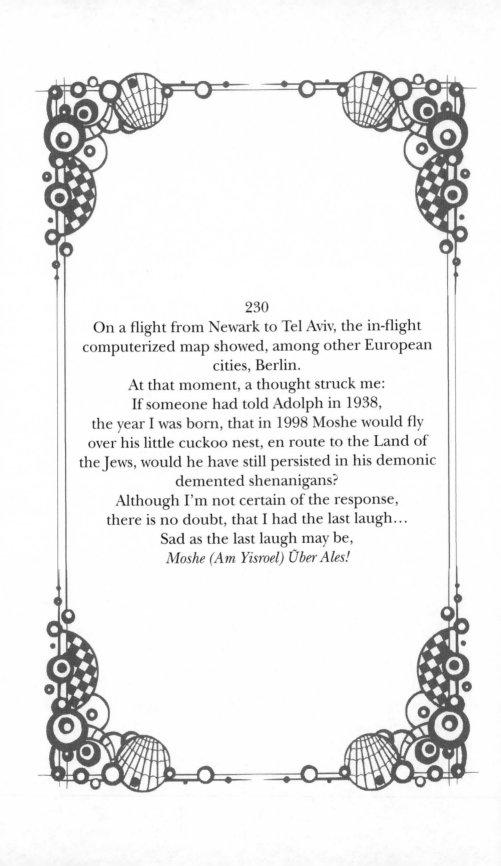

230

On a flight from Newark to Tel Aviv, the in-flight
computerized map showed, among other European
cities, Berlin.
At that moment, a thought struck me:
If someone had told Adolph in 1938,
the year I was born, that in 1998 Moshe would fly
over his little cuckoo nest, en route to the Land of
the Jews, would he have still persisted in his demonic
demented shenanigans?
Although I'm not certain of the response,
there is no doubt, that I had the last laugh…
Sad as the last laugh may be,
Moshe (Am Yisroel) Über Ales!

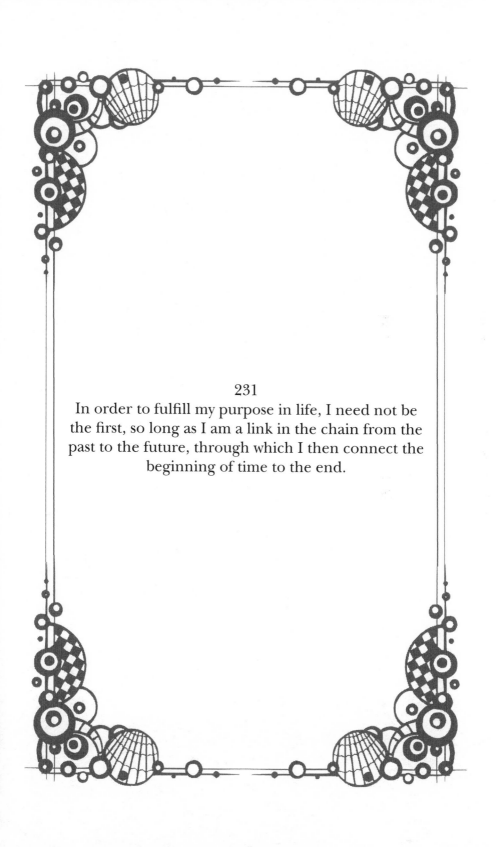

231

In order to fulfill my purpose in life, I need not be the first, so long as I am a link in the chain from the past to the future, through which I then connect the beginning of time to the end.

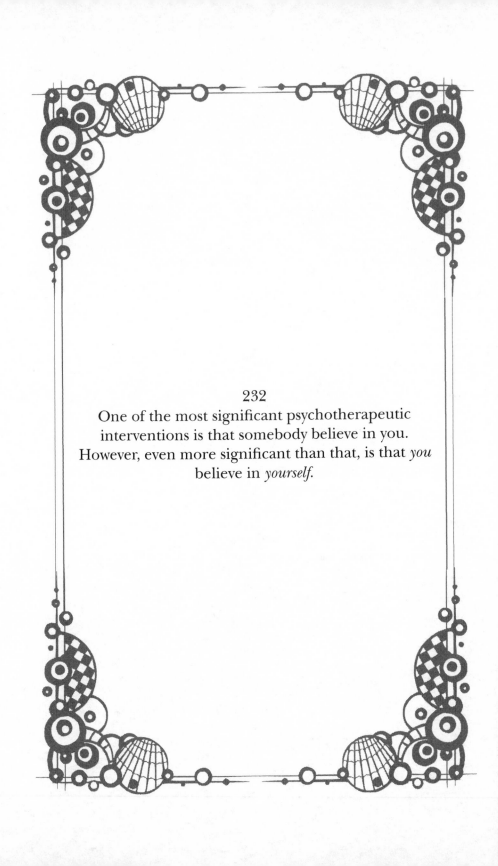

232
One of the most significant psychotherapeutic
interventions is that somebody believe in you.
However, even more significant than that, is that *you*
believe in *yourself*.

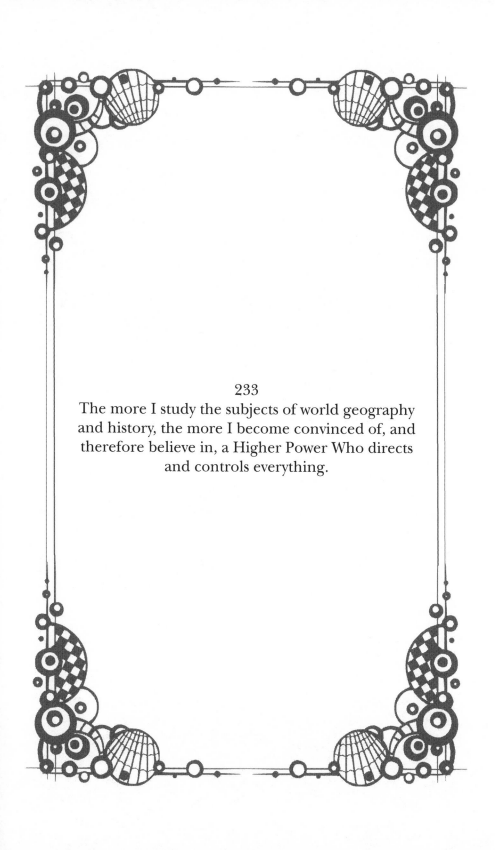

233

The more I study the subjects of world geography and history, the more I become convinced of, and therefore believe in, a Higher Power Who directs and controls everything.

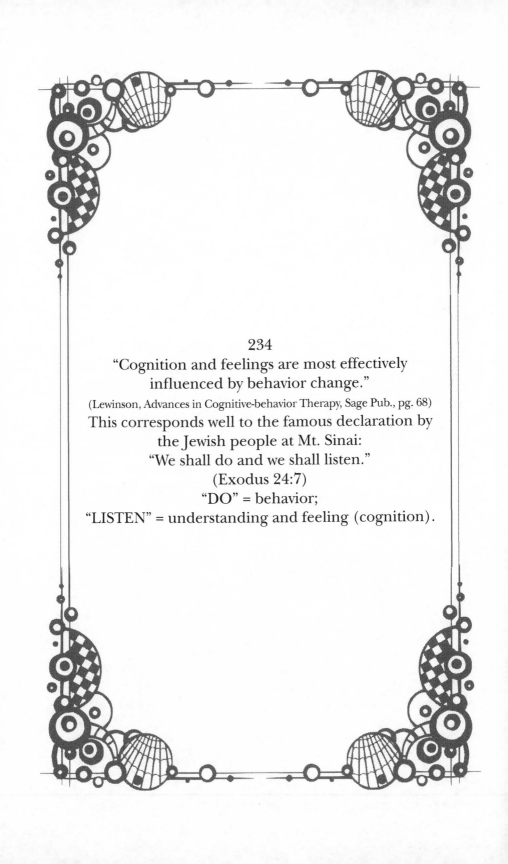

234

"Cognition and feelings are most effectively
influenced by behavior change."

(Lewinson, Advances in Cognitive-behavior Therapy, Sage Pub., pg. 68)

This corresponds well to the famous declaration by
the Jewish people at Mt. Sinai:

"We shall do and we shall listen."

(Exodus 24:7)

"DO" = behavior;

"LISTEN" = understanding and feeling (cognition).

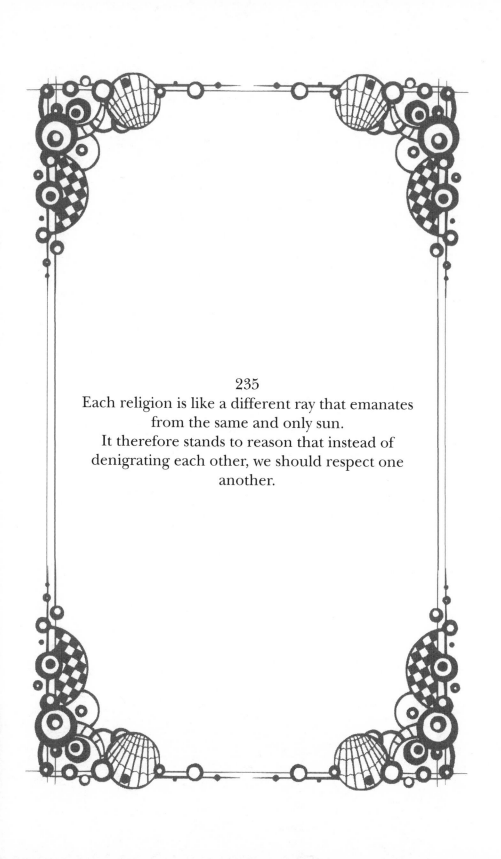

235

Each religion is like a different ray that emanates
from the same and only sun.
It therefore stands to reason that instead of
denigrating each other, we should respect one
another.

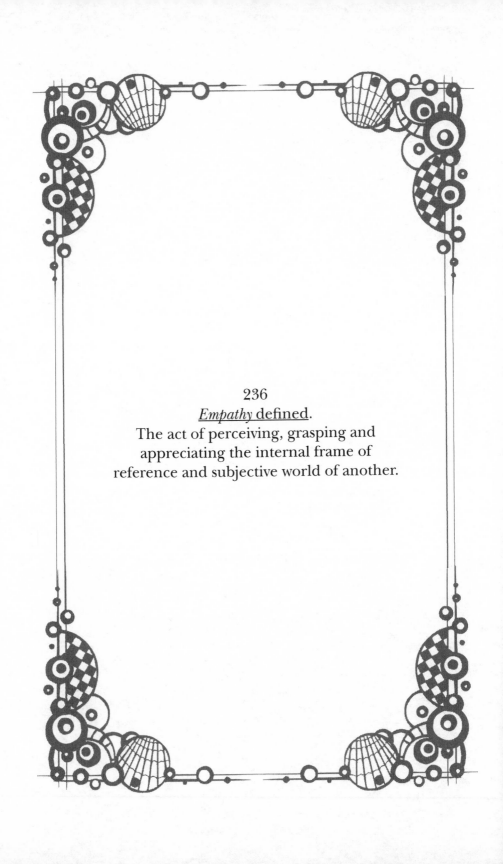

236
Empathy defined.
The act of perceiving, grasping and
appreciating the internal frame of
reference and subjective world of another.

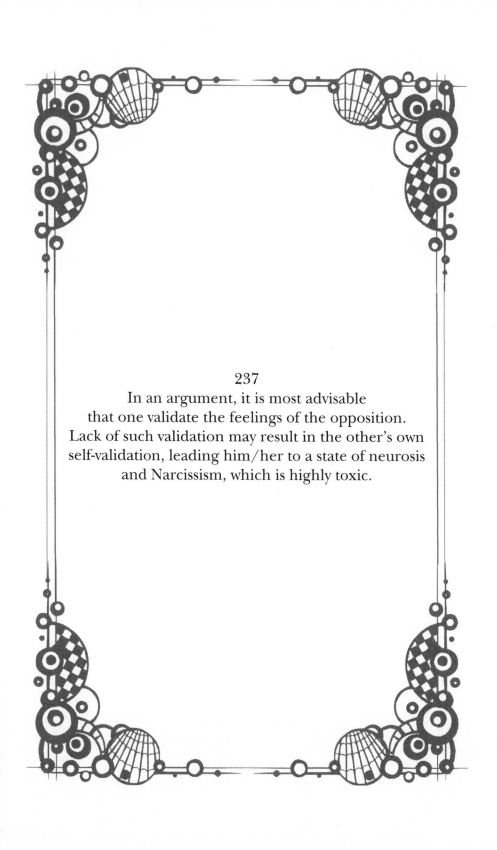

237
In an argument, it is most advisable
that one validate the feelings of the opposition.
Lack of such validation may result in the other's own
self-validation, leading him/her to a state of neurosis
and Narcissism, which is highly toxic.

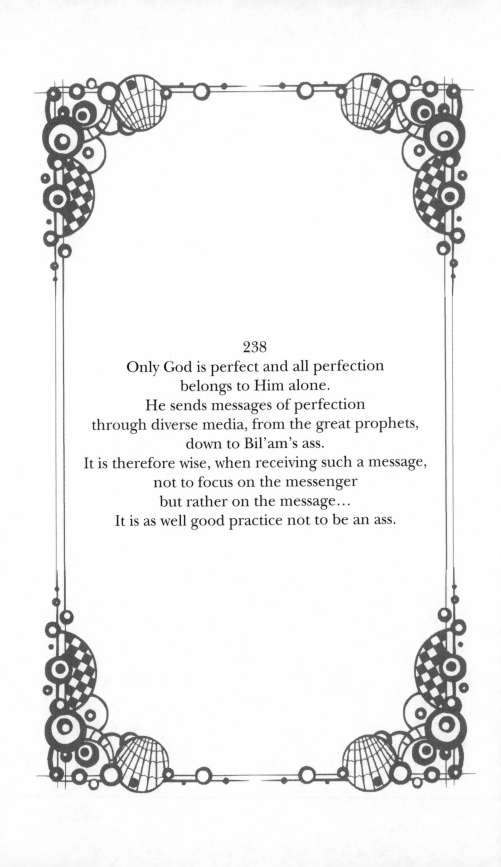

238
Only God is perfect and all perfection
belongs to Him alone.
He sends messages of perfection
through diverse media, from the great prophets,
down to Bil'am's ass.
It is therefore wise, when receiving such a message,
not to focus on the messenger
but rather on the message...
It is as well good practice not to be an ass.

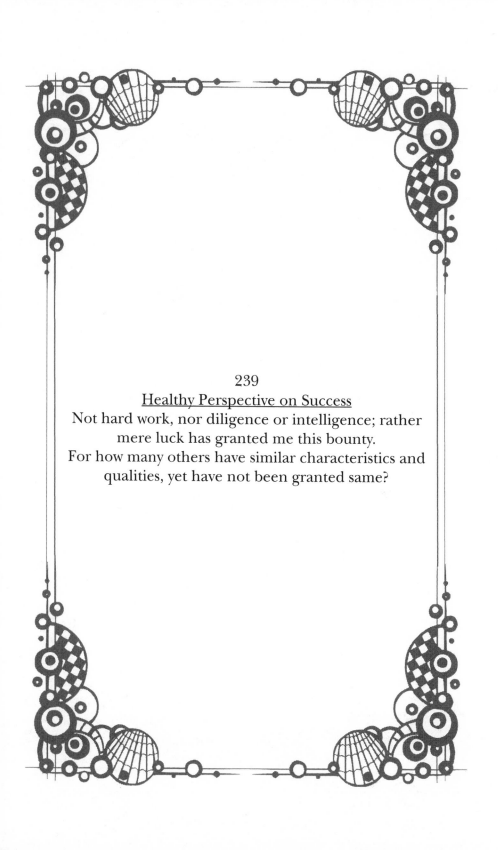

239
<u>Healthy Perspective on Success</u>
Not hard work, nor diligence or intelligence; rather
mere luck has granted me this bounty.
For how many others have similar characteristics and
qualities, yet have not been granted same?

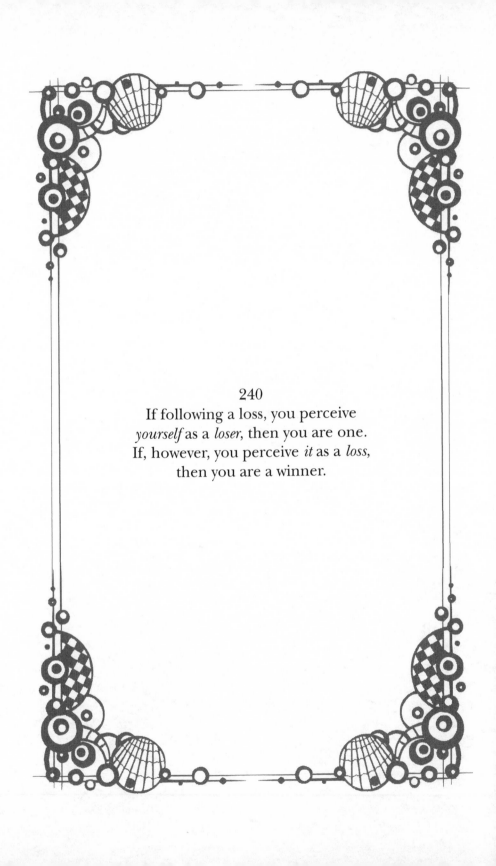

240
If following a loss, you perceive
yourself as a *loser*, then you are one.
If, however, you perceive *it* as a *loss*,
then you are a winner.

241
Those who have a need to control others, are usually
unable to control themselves.

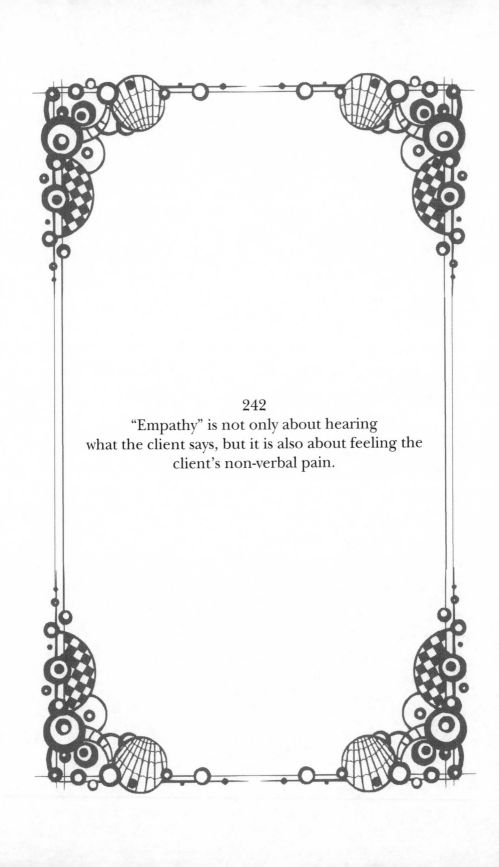

242
"Empathy" is not only about hearing
what the client says, but it is also about feeling the
client's non-verbal pain.

243
A sizeable portion of our problems is due to the
effect affecting our cognition.

244
Greatest personal pleasure is derived
from granting pleasure to others.

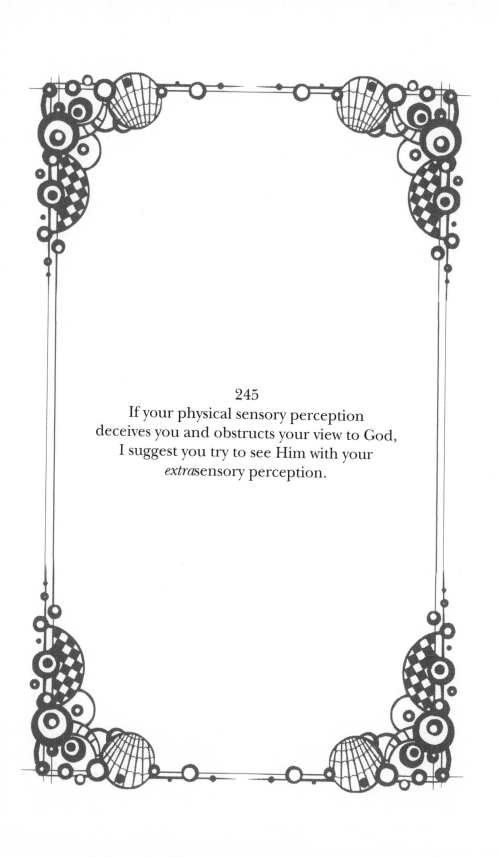

245
If your physical sensory perception
deceives you and obstructs your view to God,
I suggest you try to see Him with your
*extra*sensory perception.

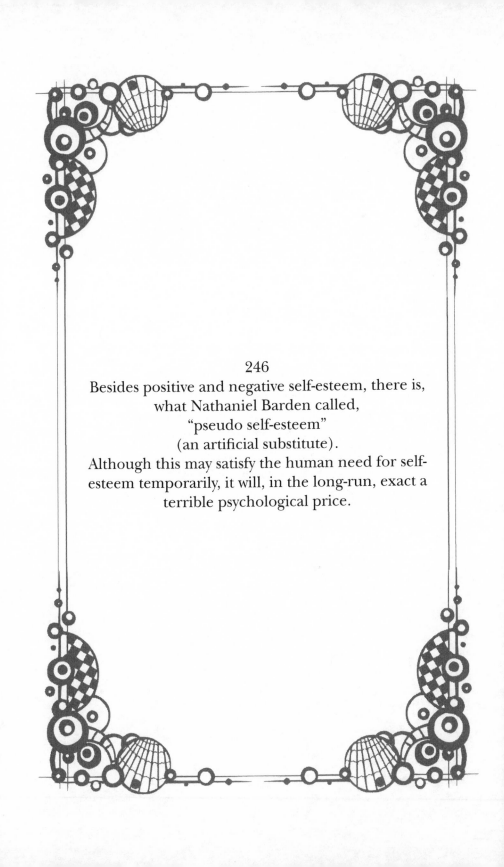

246
Besides positive and negative self-esteem, there is,
what Nathaniel Barden called,
"pseudo self-esteem"
(an artificial substitute).
Although this may satisfy the human need for self-
esteem temporarily, it will, in the long-run, exact a
terrible psychological price.

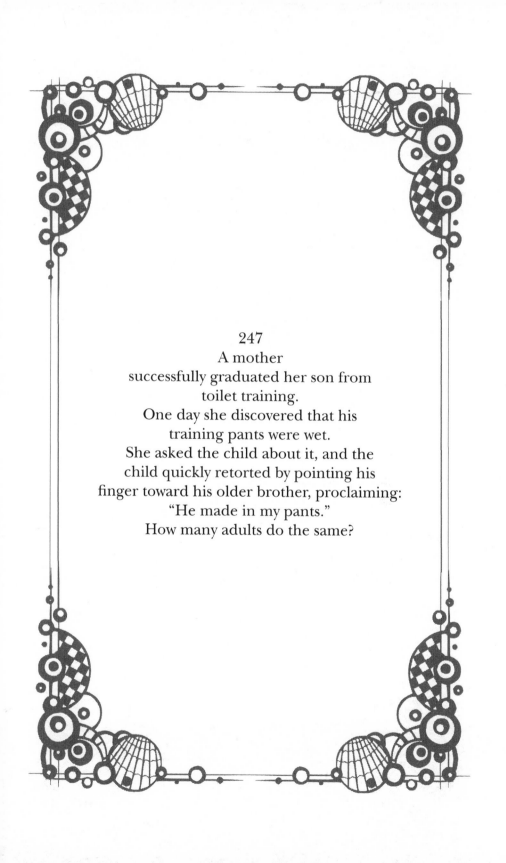

247
A mother
successfully graduated her son from
toilet training.
One day she discovered that his
training pants were wet.
She asked the child about it, and the
child quickly retorted by pointing his
finger toward his older brother, proclaiming:
"He made in my pants."
How many adults do the same?

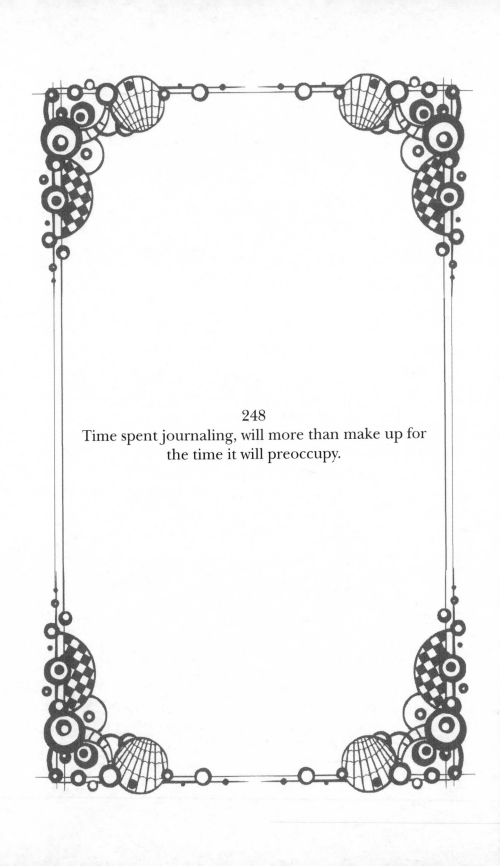

248
Time spent journaling, will more than make up for
the time it will preoccupy.

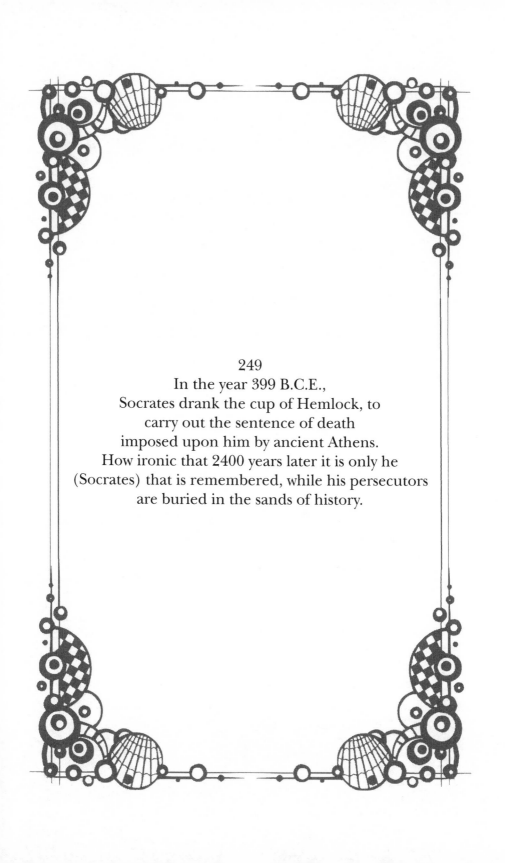

249
In the year 399 B.C.E.,
Socrates drank the cup of Hemlock, to
carry out the sentence of death
imposed upon him by ancient Athens.
How ironic that 2400 years later it is only he
(Socrates) that is remembered, while his persecutors
are buried in the sands of history.

250
You can be *for* God;
You can be *against* God;
You just cannot be *without* God.

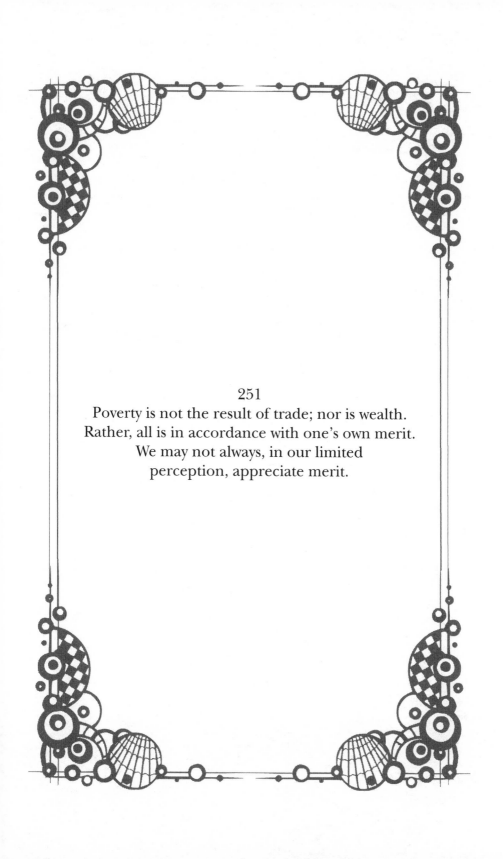

251
Poverty is not the result of trade; nor is wealth.
Rather, all is in accordance with one's own merit.
We may not always, in our limited
perception, appreciate merit.

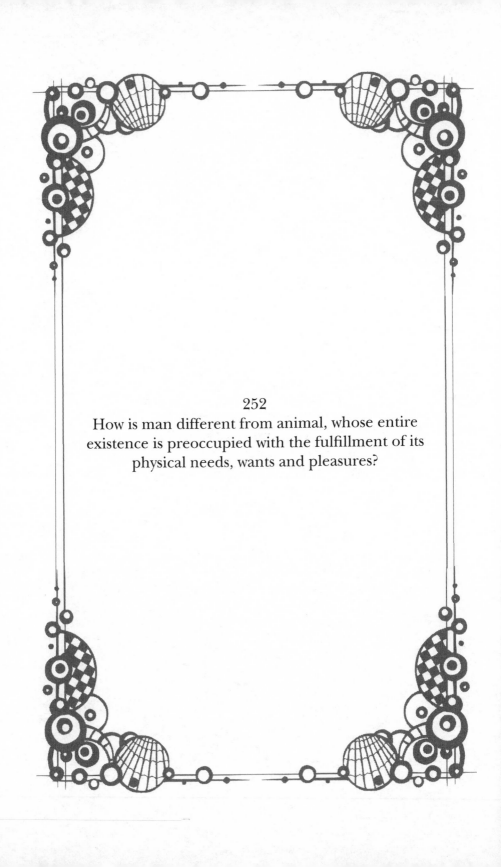

252
How is man different from animal, whose entire
existence is preoccupied with the fulfillment of its
physical needs, wants and pleasures?

253
Following my first mistake in counseling, I resolved never to sit on either my laurels... or my failures.

254
I have no enemies, only cordial opponents.
Who says I can't live with them cordially?

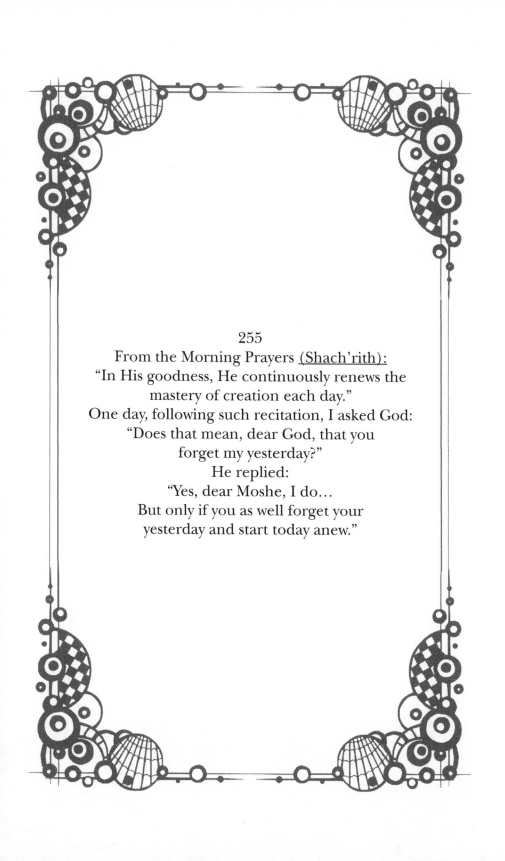

255

From the Morning Prayers <u>(Shach'rith)</u>:
"In His goodness, He continuously renews the
mastery of creation each day."
One day, following such recitation, I asked God:
"Does that mean, dear God, that you
forget my yesterday?"
He replied:
"Yes, dear Moshe, I do…
But only if you as well forget your
yesterday and start today anew."

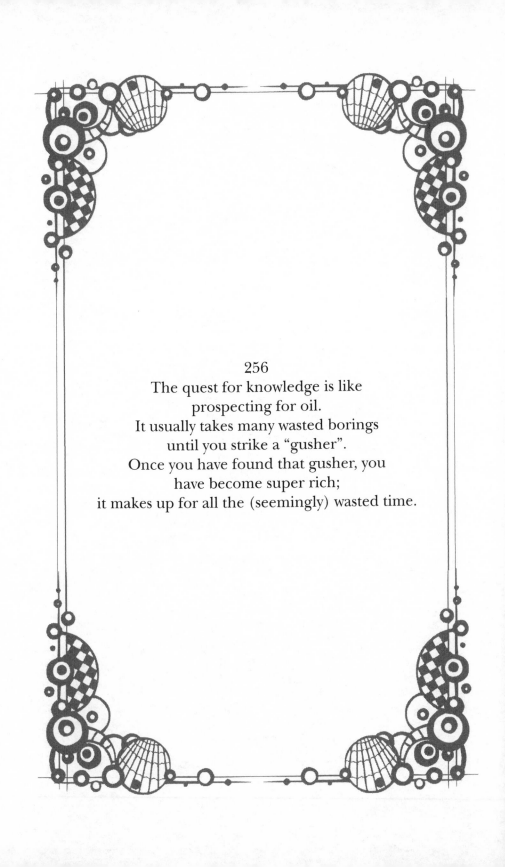

256
The quest for knowledge is like
prospecting for oil.
It usually takes many wasted borings
until you strike a "gusher".
Once you have found that gusher, you
have become super rich;
it makes up for all the (seemingly) wasted time.

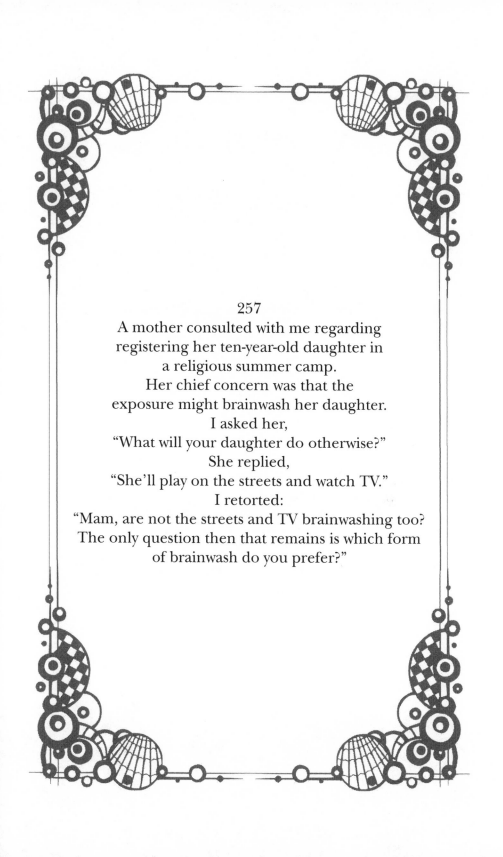

257

A mother consulted with me regarding
registering her ten-year-old daughter in
a religious summer camp.
Her chief concern was that the
exposure might brainwash her daughter.
I asked her,
"What will your daughter do otherwise?"
She replied,
"She'll play on the streets and watch TV."
I retorted:
"Mam, are not the streets and TV brainwashing too?
The only question then that remains is which form
of brainwash do you prefer?"

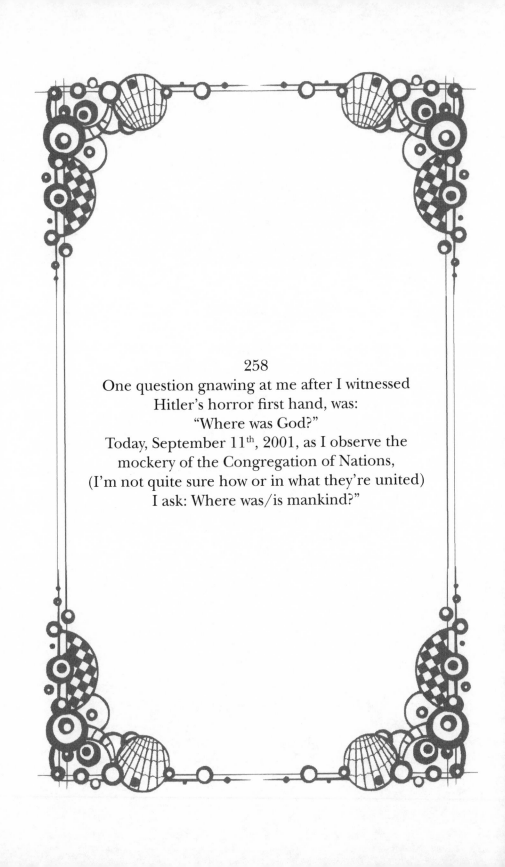

258
One question gnawing at me after I witnessed
Hitler's horror first hand, was:
"Where was God?"
Today, September 11th, 2001, as I observe the
mockery of the Congregation of Nations,
(I'm not quite sure how or in what they're united)
I ask: Where was/is mankind?"

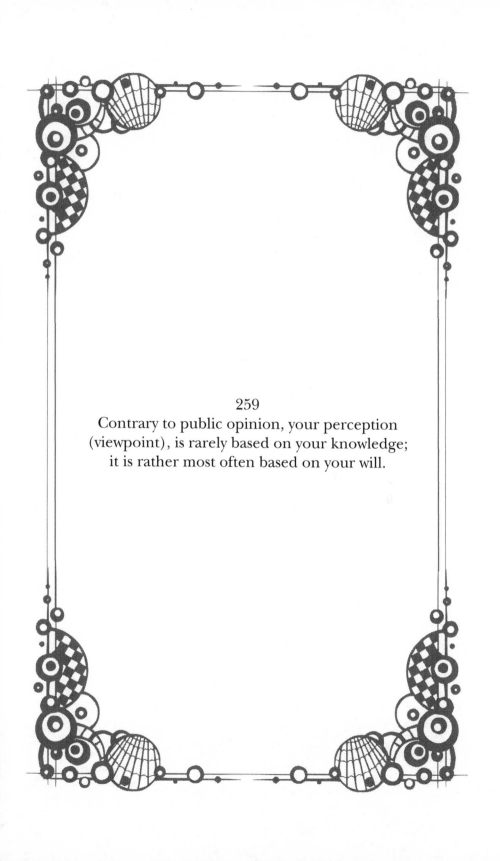

259
Contrary to public opinion, your perception
(viewpoint), is rarely based on your knowledge;
it is rather most often based on your will.

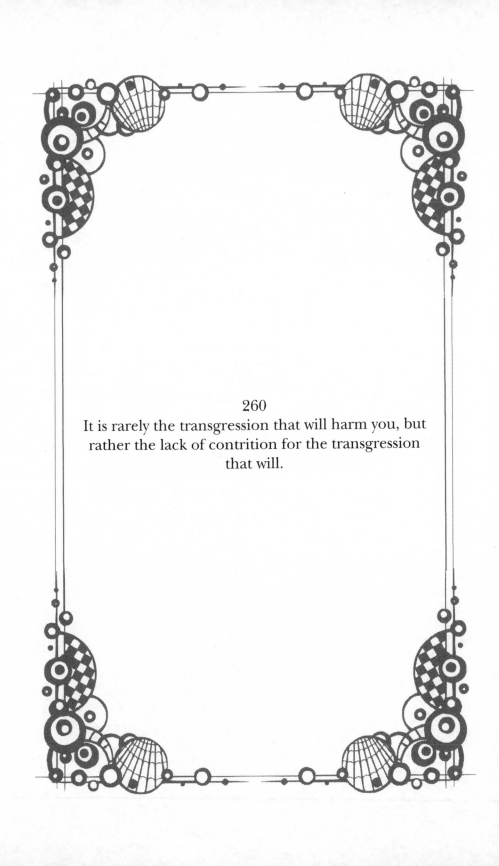

260
It is rarely the transgression that will harm you, but
rather the lack of contrition for the transgression
that will.

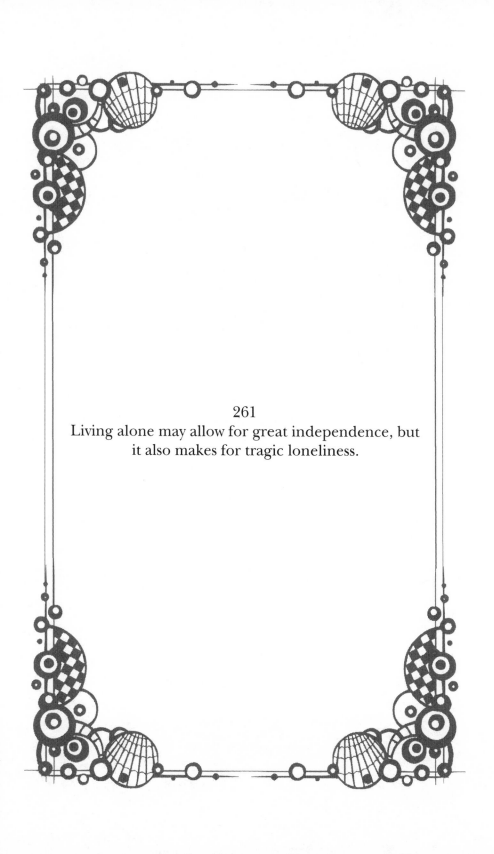

261
Living alone may allow for great independence, but
it also makes for tragic loneliness.

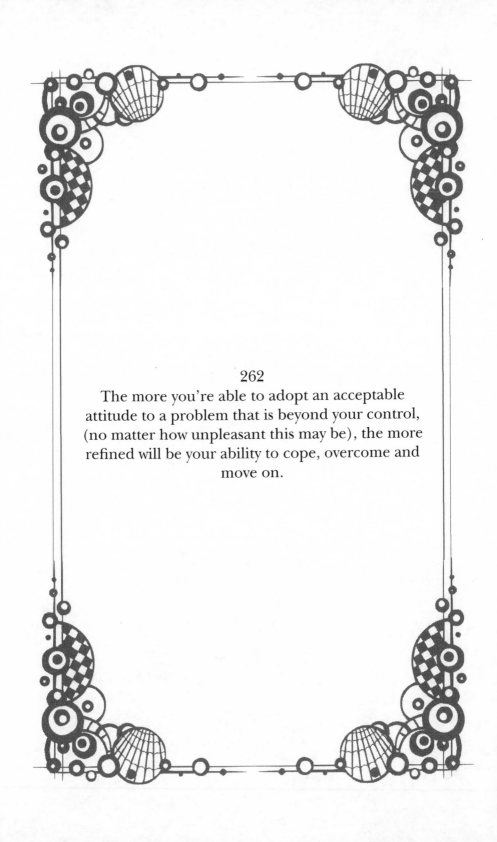

262
The more you're able to adopt an acceptable
attitude to a problem that is beyond your control,
(no matter how unpleasant this may be), the more
refined will be your ability to cope, overcome and
move on.

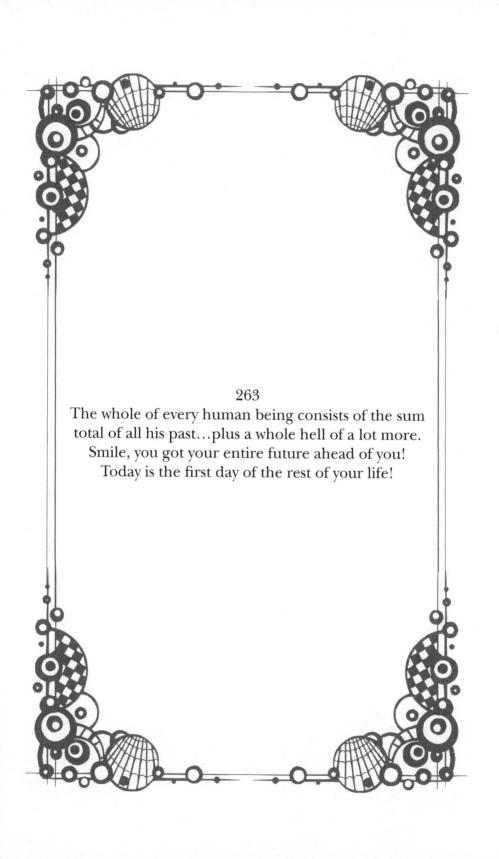

263

The whole of every human being consists of the sum
total of all his past…plus a whole hell of a lot more.
Smile, you got your entire future ahead of you!
Today is the first day of the rest of your life!

264
Sometimes, one's suffering comes from one's own
struggles against the reality of an unwanted situation.

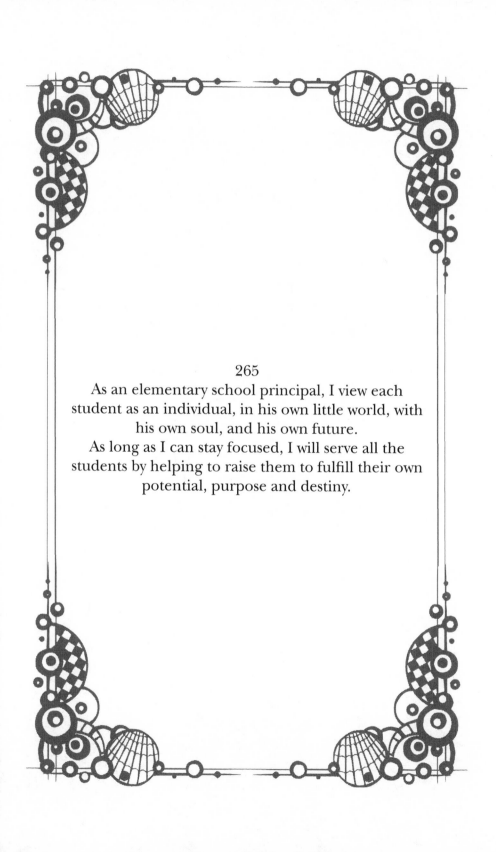

265

As an elementary school principal, I view each
student as an individual, in his own little world, with
his own soul, and his own future.

As long as I can stay focused, I will serve all the
students by helping to raise them to fulfill their own
potential, purpose and destiny.

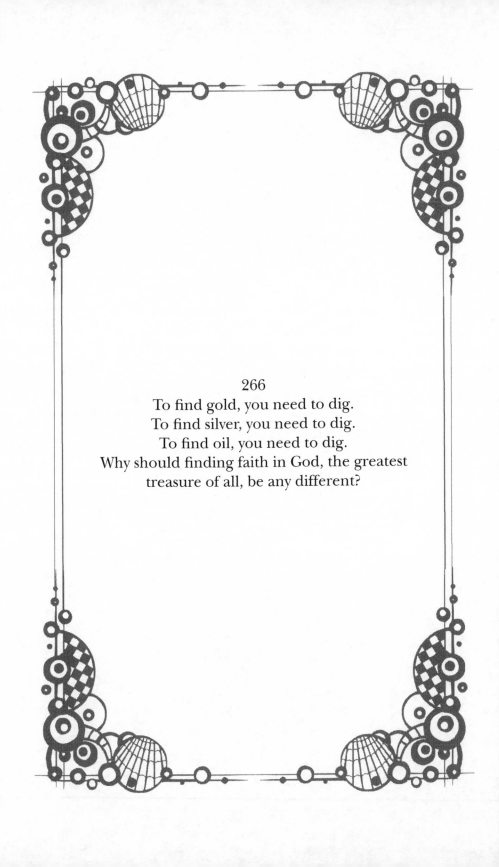

266
To find gold, you need to dig.
To find silver, you need to dig.
To find oil, you need to dig.
Why should finding faith in God, the greatest
treasure of all, be any different?

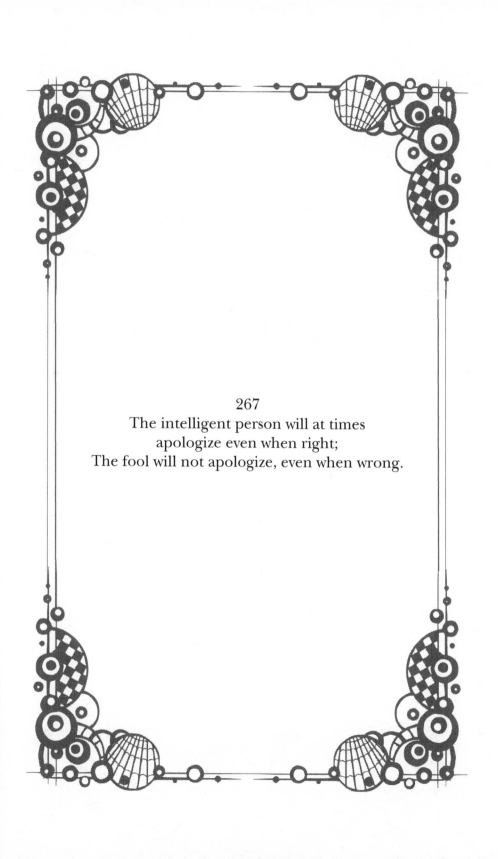

267
The intelligent person will at times
apologize even when right;
The fool will not apologize, even when wrong.

268
If you possess an
"In-your-face" personality, the last
face you will be in is the one in the mirror.

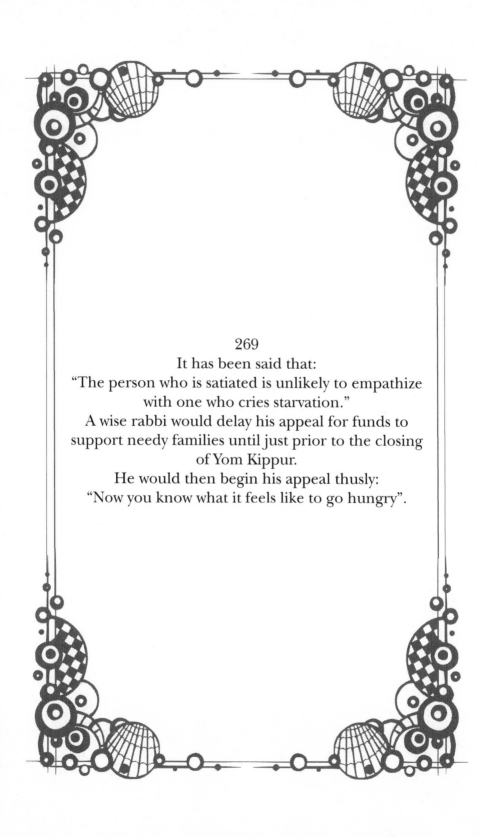

269

It has been said that:

"The person who is satiated is unlikely to empathize with one who cries starvation."

A wise rabbi would delay his appeal for funds to support needy families until just prior to the closing of Yom Kippur.

He would then begin his appeal thusly:

"Now you know what it feels like to go hungry".

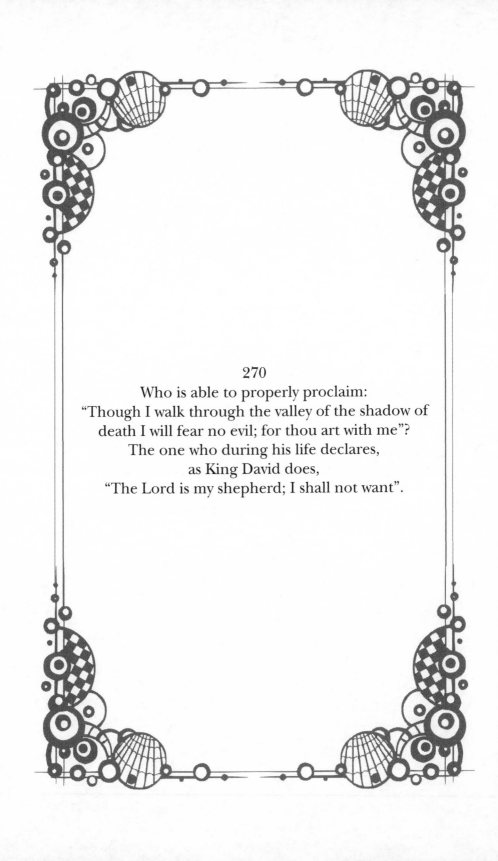

270

Who is able to properly proclaim:
"Though I walk through the valley of the shadow of
death I will fear no evil; for thou art with me"?
The one who during his life declares,
as King David does,
"The Lord is my shepherd; I shall not want".

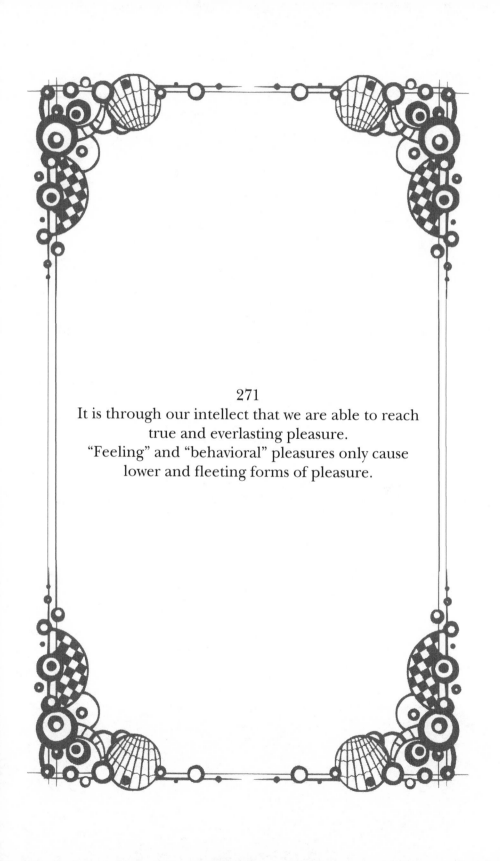

271
It is through our intellect that we are able to reach
true and everlasting pleasure.
"Feeling" and "behavioral" pleasures only cause
lower and fleeting forms of pleasure.

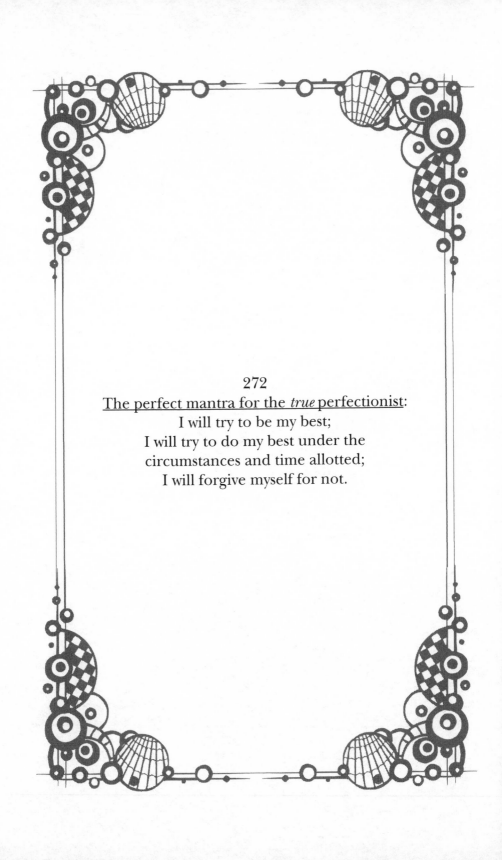

272

<u>The perfect mantra for the *true* perfectionist</u>:
I will try to be my best;
I will try to do my best under the
circumstances and time allotted;
I will forgive myself for not.

273
It may be that man cannot change.
However, man can surely *make* changes.

274
It takes time to waste time.
On the other hand, sometimes one
needs to waste time in order to maximize it.

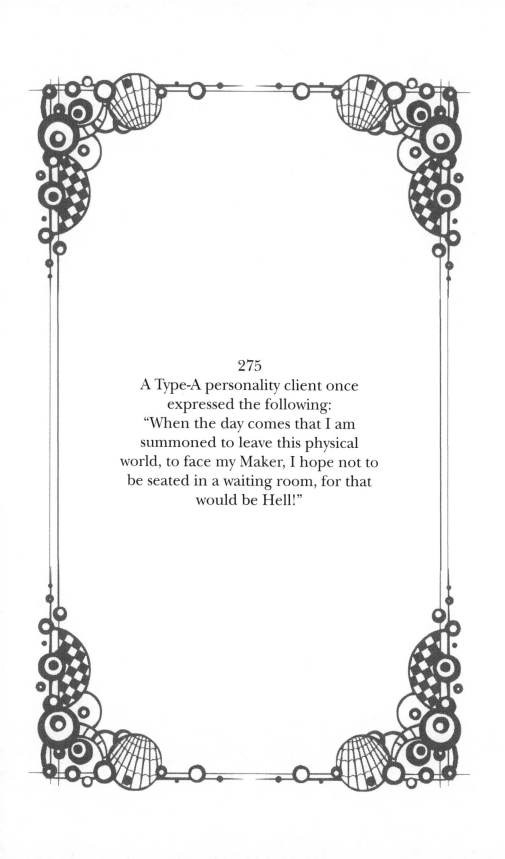

275

A Type-A personality client once
expressed the following:
"When the day comes that I am
summoned to leave this physical
world, to face my Maker, I hope not to
be seated in a waiting room, for that
would be Hell!"

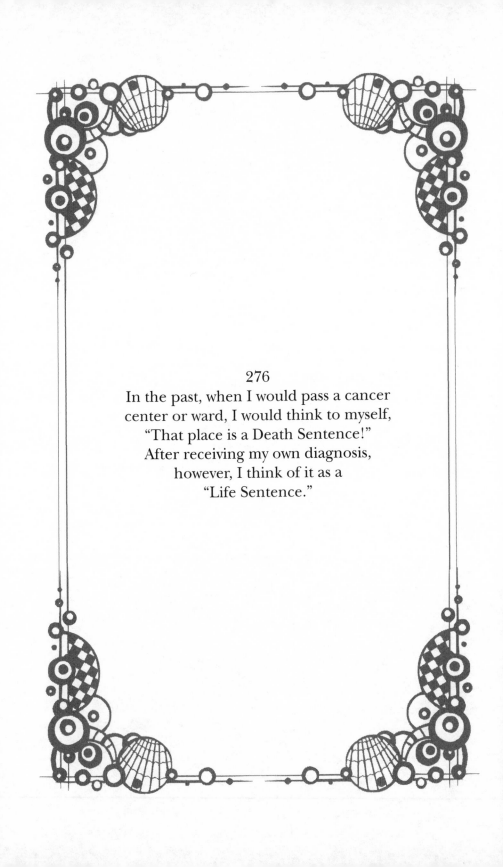

276

In the past, when I would pass a cancer
center or ward, I would think to myself,
"That place is a Death Sentence!"
After receiving my own diagnosis,
however, I think of it as a
"Life Sentence."

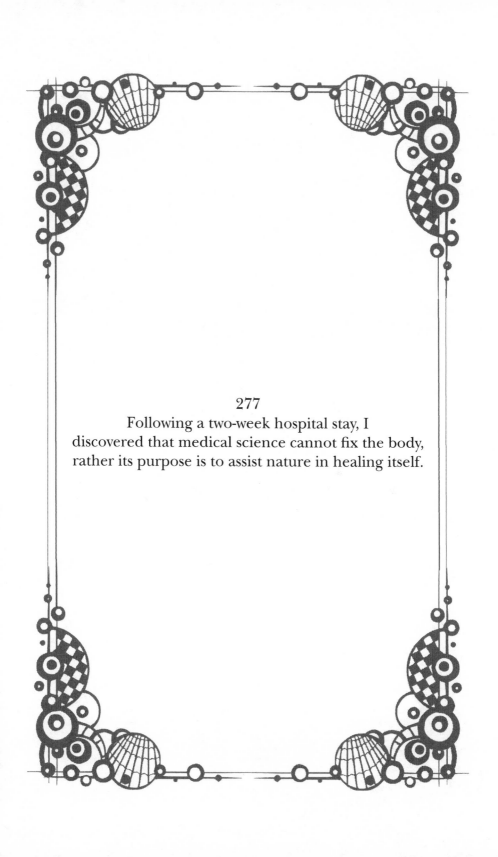

277
Following a two-week hospital stay, I
discovered that medical science cannot fix the body,
rather its purpose is to assist nature in healing itself.

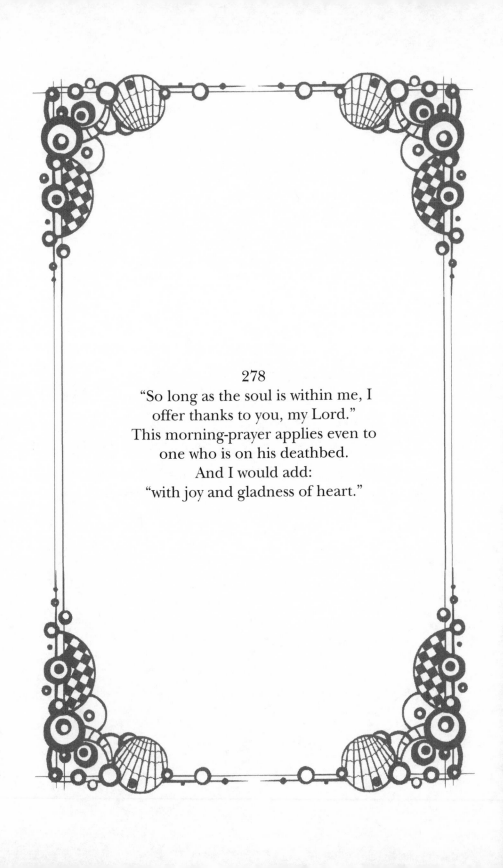

278
"So long as the soul is within me, I
offer thanks to you, my Lord."
This morning-prayer applies even to
one who is on his deathbed.
And I would add:
"with joy and gladness of heart."

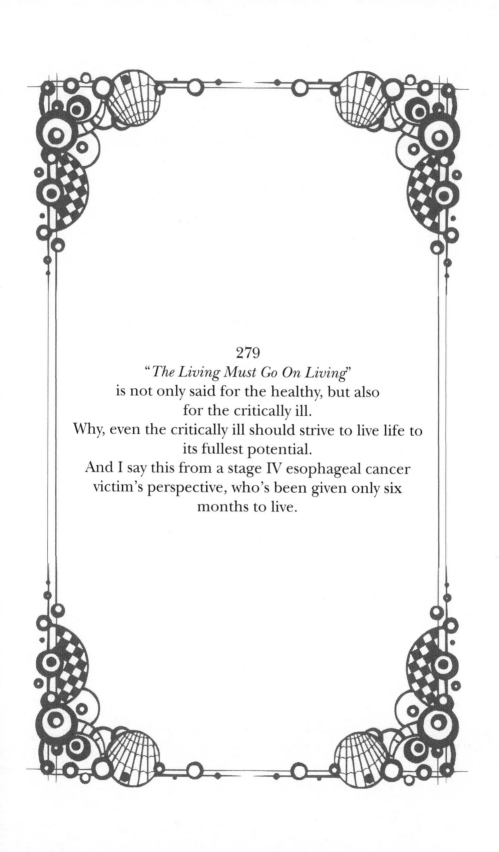

279

"The Living Must Go On Living"
is not only said for the healthy, but also
for the critically ill.
Why, even the critically ill should strive to live life to
its fullest potential.
And I say this from a stage IV esophageal cancer
victim's perspective, who's been given only six
months to live.

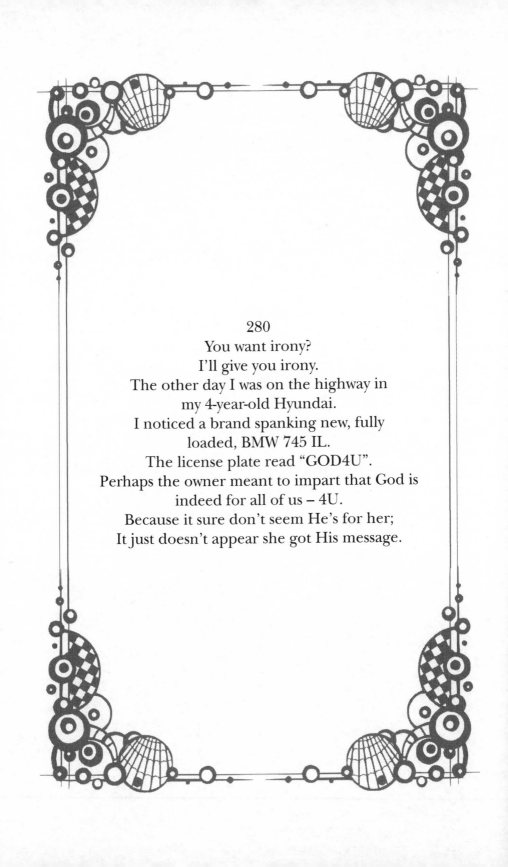

280
You want irony?
I'll give you irony.
The other day I was on the highway in
my 4-year-old Hyundai.
I noticed a brand spanking new, fully
loaded, BMW 745 IL.
The license plate read "GOD4U".
Perhaps the owner meant to impart that God is
indeed for all of us – 4U.
Because it sure don't seem He's for her;
It just doesn't appear she got His message.

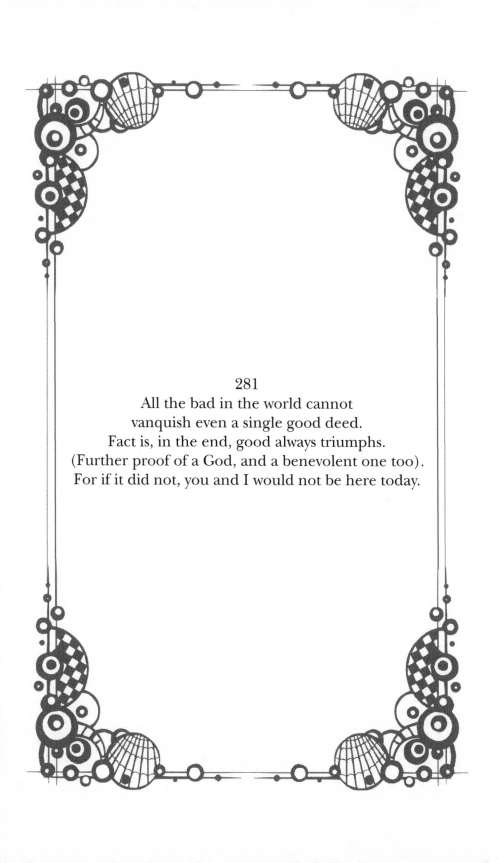

281
All the bad in the world cannot
vanquish even a single good deed.
Fact is, in the end, good always triumphs.
(Further proof of a God, and a benevolent one too).
For if it did not, you and I would not be here today.

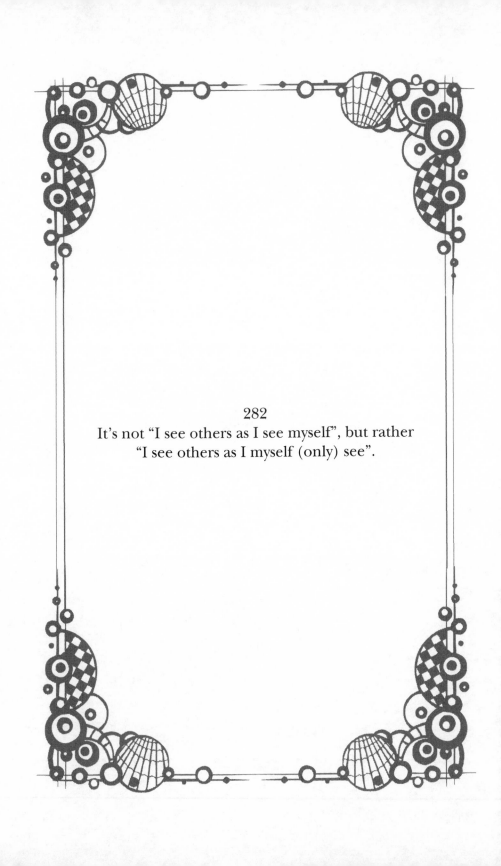

282
It's not "I see others as I see myself", but rather
"I see others as I myself (only) see".

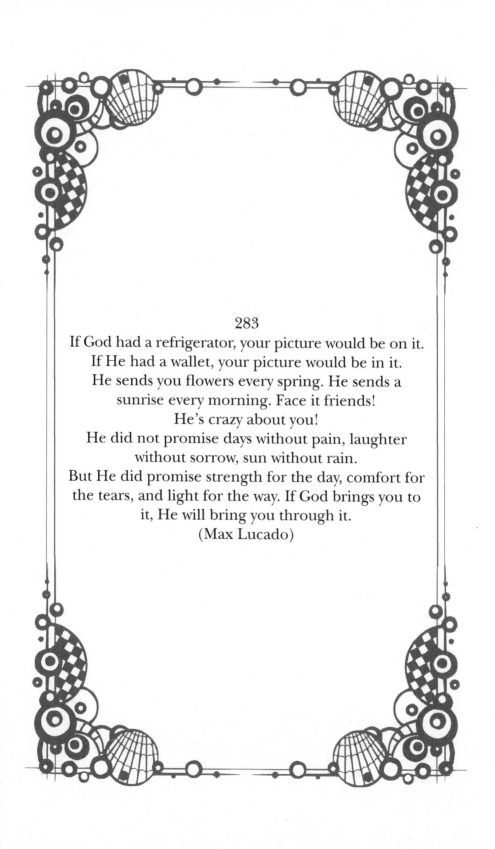

283

If God had a refrigerator, your picture would be on it.
If He had a wallet, your picture would be in it.
He sends you flowers every spring. He sends a
sunrise every morning. Face it friends!
He's crazy about you!
He did not promise days without pain, laughter
without sorrow, sun without rain.
But He did promise strength for the day, comfort for
the tears, and light for the way. If God brings you to
it, He will bring you through it.
(Max Lucado)

APPENDIX

Thoughts on preparation for my first Chemotherapy treatment for Stage IV Esophageal Cancer
June 16, 2003/16 Sivan 5763

1. I thank God, (exalted and hallowed be His Great Name), for having granted me life, sustained me and enabled me to reach this time in my life; from (physically) saving me from the Holocaust to the establishment of a family I am so proud of, and to the other accomplishments in my life.

2. I always feel that I am in God's Hands and in His protection. Nothing can, nor will happen to me, unless it is His will, which is perfectly fine with me. I accept His judgments with happiness and joy.

3. I want to thank God for having guided my steps in securing, what I believe is, the best medical team, with doctors that are both humble and positive.

4. I want to thank God for blessing me with such a great family support system; this must be one of the best family support groups in the world, if not the best.

5. I want to thank God for the larger support system from one end of the world to the other, for their blessings, prayers, thoughts and good wishes.

The following is what I have decided to do for myself,
(for God helps those who help themselves).

1. I have prepared my mind and subconscious with a theme song to go along with the chemotherapy and my road to recovery. "*Tracht Gut Vet Zayn gut*" (Think Positive and It Shall Be So).

2. I have prepared a victory song, with the following lyrics (motto): "*Fight with joy, and ye shall overcome*".

3. I have told myself that I am going to take a page out of the Bush Book and "*SHOCK AND AWE*" the cancer into the submission.

285

LIFE AND DEATH IS IN THE POWER OF THE TONGUE
(Proverbs 18:21)
A tale of two patients with the same diagnosis –
Stage IV Espophageal Cancer:

A's doctor: "I am a straight shooter. Chemotherapy 'could' help. If you decide to go ahead with chemotherapy, it would be highly advisable to start as soon as you are comfortably able, because it is fast growing. Surgery is not an option because the cancer has metastasized. Chemotherapy is effective in approximately 35-40% of patients, (the term "effective" must also be qualified)." Doctor gave patient 6 to 12 months.

B's doctor spent three hours with the patient, reviewing and studying all of patient's records, tests, biopsies, MRIs, etc. He finally returned with his plan of attack. Doctor also assured patient that if the recommended method is ineffective, there are other options. Doctor B was also honest and did not paint an unrealistic picture for patient, but simultaneously expressed sincere care, kindness and concern, and did so with an amazing sense of optimism and hope, not found in the medical field.

EPILOGUE:
Patient "A" left doctor depressed; he was dead six months later.
Patient "B" was still around 22 months later.

MARRIAGE: A POEM
(by Yaffa Rabin, my eldest daughter)

As you start off together in your new life,
follow this way, to avoid strife.

This is the time when all the advice,
can mold a marriage of a husband and wife.

Marriage is the chance for life's greatest fulfillment,
companionship and love to which there is no comparison.

Marriage is the most wonderful gift,
developed and used as God sees fit.

Marriage is more precious than diamonds and gold,
be sure to perfect and preserve it until you grow old.

To share each other's lives, feelings and goals,
to come out of yourselves and help each other grow.

To use all your potential to be the best you can be,
as you climb together on this lifelong tree.

A relationship is precious, unique and dear,
it's developed with much thoughtfulness emotion and tears.

It's expressions of sharing both hardship and joy,
it's being able to act like a little girl or boy.

It's being accepted for who you are,
this safe feeling will carry each of you far.

It's laughing together at things that are funny,
and planning together on budgeting money.

It's an investment which if tended well,
will be worth the wedding bells.

Be sure to learn together and develop a bond,
of each other ye shall grow fond.

When things settle down, two people realize,
that although they're married, it's okay to see the world through different eyes.

Always communicate come what may,
but be careful in the underlying message you relay.

Everyone has feelings and deserves respect,
support your spouse and show care, it'll have an effect.

Don't be sarcastic, be open and honest,
say what you feel, and the marriage will be calmest.

Treat your partner as you want to be treated,
loved at all times, even when defeated.

For after all, marriage is not a war,
nor is it a struggle for power to see who gets more.

The freedom to express wishes and feeling,
to unite as one whole in order to have meaning.

Make sure you talk, but listen too,
You'd want the same be done unto you.

But how easy it is to make that mistake,
of being nasty or cold, just to save face.

There's no need though with a loved one so close,
one can apologize to the person one loves most.

And you're never lost, you always gain,
because now you are closer and the friendship remains.

Never assume your spouse should have known,
just be open and sharing and help them be caring.

Don't look to change your spouse's way,
dwell on their fine points and brighten their day.

Changes come slowly, but only through talk,
that is loving and caring and constructively taught.

The closeness you build in all areas of life,
will spill over to your home and spread joyful light.

Moshe's Philosophy (Theology) of True Life

6 Tammuz 5703/ July 6, 2003

On April 25, 2003, one day following the Passover holiday, I received a diagnosis of incurable and metastasized cancer. I have been asked many times how I accepted the news, and how I maintain a positive mood and even a sense of humor.

When I got the news, I first thanked God profusely for having granted me life, for having sustained me and brought me to this time. I thanked God for having saved me from WWII. I also thanked Him for saving me from severe pneumonia and pleurisy in 1980, and later from a colon scare in 1995 and prostate scare in 1998. I then counted my blessings of having raised a wonderful family, reflected on my many life accomplishments, and on the manuscripts I have authored and published.

When I got the seemingly dreadful news, this is what it felt like. I imagined that God tapped me on the shoulder and called out "Moshe! Moshe!", to which I turned around and replied: "Here I am, my Lord. What is it that you wish of me? I will do anything with the greatest joy and gladness of heart". "I have your next assignment", He said. For me, the path was clear. I had a test to overcome. I snapped out of my séance.

I then began to bargain with God for further years of life. I expressed great hope and faith that God will be with me. My saying is:

"When control over a situation escapes me, my faith kicks in. I place control in the hands of a "Higher Power" and, as a result, my anguish dissipates."

As for reality therapy, I began putting my affairs in order. There were many things to take care of. I even went so far as to acquire a burial plot.

In order to answer the question of how I keep a positive mood, I would like to share with you some basic principles and truths. These have helped me deal with things throughout my life, and are especially helpful in my current situation. These principles can be categorized into three basic fundamentals:

- Faith
- Relationship
- Humility & Gratitude

I will expound on each of these, and explain their relevance to a good attitude and a sense of humor in the face of adversity.

Recognizing that I was faced with a test, I took to the Torah and gleaned some lessons from Abraham, whom God tested ten times. Abraham passed them all with great success. Abraham became the most famous individual in the world. His name has even been adopted by most of the world's cultures and religions. Did Abraham know he was being tested? Did he know he was going to pass these tests? Did he even know that these were tests? It is only in hindsight that his success has been realized.

Abraham's final test was when G-d ordered him to sacrifice his son, Isaac. How do you imagine Abraham felt? Do you think it was easy for him? Yet, we find that Abraham acceded to God's desires with great alacrity. Abraham was able to do so because he developed a relationship with God that superseded all of Abraham's personal desires and intellect.

In our daily prayers we beseech God, "please do *not* bring us to sin, nor to transgression or iniquity, nor to *tests*." But it has also been said, that God gives each person according to one's ability to bear and endure. The word "test" in Hebrew is "*nais*", which also means a raised flag, meaning that through passing a test, the individual is raised to a higher status.

To quote Tanya, *Igeret Hakodesh,* chapter 11:

The purpose of man's creation in this world is to test him by trials, to ascertain what is in his heart: Whether he will turn his heart towards the other gods, namely the passions of the body which evolve from the *sitra achra* (*dark side*) and desire these, or whether his desire and wish is to live the true life which evolves from the Living God.

Nobody says that a test is easy, but just as the more one exercises and the more the muscles hurt, the stronger those muscles become, so too with challenges God places in our paths. I regard my latest malady as a "test" from God and therefore I am reacting in accordance with the above.

Now, to detail the "Three Points":

1. FAITH

For years, I have been incorporating philosophies from the volume "*Chovot Ha'Levavoth, Duties of the Heart*" (*Bachaya Ibn Paquda, Sha'ar Ha'Bitachon*), which I recommend everyone read, who writes as follows:

> ......Another advantage of trust in God is that the business person grieves little if his wares remain on his shelves, or a business transaction is delayed, or he cannot collect an account due him, or if he falls sick; since he is conscious that the Creator, blessed be He, arranges his affairs better than he himself is be able to, and chooses what is in the businessman's best interest better than he can, as it is said, "Upon God alone, I my soul, do thou wait, for my expectation is from Him (Psalms 62:6)."

> A further advantage is that he rejoices, whatever the situation, even if it is contrary to his nature, because he always trusts that God will not do anything except what is good in all things, just as a tender mother acts toward her infant child – bathing it, putting on its diaper gently, tying a band around its body or loosening it – all without regard to the infant's will, as King David writes: "Surely I have stilled and quieted my soul like a weaned child with his mother; my soul is with me like a weaned child (Psalms 131:2)"

> ..... When this will have become clear to a human being, and his recognition of the verity of God's loving kindness will have become strong, he will put trust in Him, give himself up completely to Him, leave the guidance of his life to Him, never suspect the justice of His sentence nor get angry at what He has chosen for him, as David writes: "I will lift up the cup of salvation and call upon the name of the Lord (Psalms 116:13); I found trouble and sorrow, then called I upon the name of the Lord (Ibid 116:3-4)"

> ..... It was because of the exalted Creator's compassion for man that He caused him to trouble himself with secular affairs in this

world and with His salvation in the hereafter, so that he should be occupied therewith throughout his life and not seek what he does not need and to which he cannot attain with his understanding, as for instance, knowledge of the origin, and final end of the Universe.

After becoming aware of, and studying, this profound concept, one might think that you must be a "Holy Person" in order to develop a strong faith in God that will sustain you through all the trials, tribulations and tests of life. This is _NOT_ the case. Faith in God follows relationship building and development procedures just as relationships develop between man and fellow man, between husband and wife, between parent and child, especially father and child, since we address God as our Father in Heaven.

2. RELATIONSHIP

Here are some rules in building and developing relationships:
* Communicate; verbalize your feelings.
* Be non-judgmental.
* Don't criticize, condemn or complain.
* Congruence – be truthful.
* Unconditional positive regard.

The meaning of relationship is that both participants give and receive. In our relationship with God, we must recognize and be gracious toward God for the fulfillment of our daily needs; that we have health, food, a roof over our heads, a job (if we have one), air to breathe, etc.

It is important to remember, that the more humble we are, the happier we will be with what we have. That is not to say that we should not ask for more. But if we don't get what _we_ want, we should realize that this is God's will and we ought to be thankful for that.

Most aspects of a human relationship are the same as our relationship with God. There is, however, one difference. We cannot actually see God in the flesh. Yet we need to learn to feel and perceive Him as true reality. This is done through "awareness" of Him.

If you *don't* see God with your physical *sensory perception,* I suggest you try to see him with your *intellectual perception,* as did the biblical prophets, like Moses, and others. The scripture actually refers to that intellectual perception as vision. It has even been said, and the sources are rather convincing, that Moses' intellectual vision was so refined that he 'physically' saw God.

3. GRATITUDE & HUMILITY

I learned a lesson from our forefather, Jacob, that we need to be appreciative and grateful and not complain. When Jacob descended to Egypt, his son Joseph brought him to King Pharaoh. The King asked Jacob how old he was, to which Jacob replied, "I am 130 years old. Few and bad have been the days of the years of my life." *(Genesis, 47:9)* Jacob expressed his life's complaints.

The Midrash tells us that the number of words Jacob verbalized in his complaint totaled 33. God decreed that each word would cost him one year of his life. Hence Jacob lived to age 147, whereas his father, Isaac, lived to 180 years.

If you feel that life is unfair, I suggest that you humble yourself so that you may be able to comprehend the following quote from Prophet Isaiah:

"For my thoughts are not your thoughts; neither are your ways my ways, says the Lord." (Isaiah, 54:8)

God's plan is way beyond our ability to grasp, but since He is the source of life and goodness, everything that comes from Him must be good, whether we see it and feel it or not.

The core meaning of awareness of God is having "<u>knowledge</u>" of the existence of something you don't see or feel. And again, you *don't* have to be a "holy person" to do this. Everyone can do it. The most basic criterion to reach this goal is "gratitude", which comes from "humility".

"Humility" is the hallmark of Moses, *(besides Abraham and King David).* Moses was the most humble of all men. The Messiah will also possess an abundant and unprecedented sum of humility. He will teach Torah to the Patriarchs, and to Moses, yet he will be the ultimate in humility and self-nullification, for he will also teach simple folk.

This is in contrast to the Gentile Kings of the Late Bronze Age, the Iron Age and of Classical Antiquity:

Nebuchadnezzar – *I will resemble the Supreme One.*

Sanheirob – *Who among all the gods of these lands?*

Hiram – *I am a god, I sat on the throne of God.*

Here are a few basic pointers:

1. God represents only good. If something occurs that *appears* to be a tragedy, it emanates from the concealed part of God. Therefore, when we ask for God's blessings, we add the words "from the revealed part of God", asking for good that is recognizable to us as good.

2. Review tragedies that occurred in your lifetime, and examine to see if there was a "silver lining". If not, see King David's praise of the Lord :

"*Everything that happens does so because it fits into the divine scheme of the universe, and therefore is bound to be good*". (Psalms 145:9)

In a tragic time, rather than *blame* Him for your predicament, consider the tragedy a *test* from Above.

Develop gratitude, and <u>practice it!</u> A person must review his life and find the blessings and miracles that he has previously taken for granted and considered to be mere coincidence. It is best when one verbalizes the gratitude. Expressing gratitude aloud to yourself or others is a powerful means of internalizing those feelings.

The more humble you are, the easier it will be to find the goodness and happiness you have, in spite of all the non-happy situations and sad life travails you may have experienced. Through humility, you will not just thank God, but you will "be thankful" as well, and thus acquire a positive attitude to help you succeed in overcoming life's greatest obstacles and challenges.

King Solomon, who lived 3,000 years ago, made some statements, which are true and relevant today. For example, in Ecclesiastics the great king writes:

"*All that has been, will be; and all that has been done will be done again; and there is nothing new under the sun*". *(1:9)*

Three millennia later, looking around and studying the world, it appears that anything that seems to be new, is not really new. It has only been developed from natural resources, which were in existence before and are in existence now, but nothing is new.

When King Solomon talks about life he writes the following:

"*Vanity of vanities, said Koheleth (King Solomon), vanity of vanities, all is vanity*".

The accepted meaning of the word "vanity" is: "worthlessness". This refers to a situation where the objective is reachable, but hardly worth the effort. (The physical and material is a reachable objective, but on its own is not worthwhile.)

Koheleth writes, "all is vanity" (tongue-in-cheek). Because King Solomon stresses that life is to be enjoyed, and that man is held responsible and accountable for all his deeds. Certainly, one as wise as King Solomon, who enjoyed life and had everything in the world that man could possibly want, and urges others to enjoy life, couldn't possibly have believed that life is vanity! However, the obvious answer is that those who see life as *only* a race for material possessions, will not find meaning in life, for they do not aspire to higher values. Such a person sees only inequality among men, monotony and routine in nature, and frustration in the human struggle. To him, of course, all is vanity – void of meaning.

In addition, King Solomon writes the following:

"*What profit has man of all his labor under the sun?*"(Ibid. 1:3)

If "*under the sun there is no profit,*" is there then profit *above* the sun? *Koheleth* is referring to *under the sun* as the material world. If one takes the "*under-the-sun*" point of view, and only believes what he sees or understands in this world, then life's labor has no profit. Life is subject to haphazard natural circumstances, follows no logical pattern, and is replete with injustices and inequality. Only when man reaches outside of the physical realm, "*above the sun,*" is he able to find meaning in life and living. Only the spiritual and metaphysical give profit and purpose to life and living.

As a result of faith, relationship, gratitude and humility, you will eventually develop a sense of great security, as never before, and ultimately a sense of humor. You will always feel safe and sound, knowing that your life has been full of "above the sun" – life that has meaning and lasting value.

Looking around and seeing that most of the people occupy their lives with "under the sun" matters, which are worthless and futile, I find it humorous that after an entire life of 80 or 90 years, they have nothing to show for it. What do they have? Where are they going? What are they taking along?

It's time to ask yourself:

Where am I going? What valuables do I truly possess? Whatever I do possess, where am I taking it to? Most importantly, what legacy am I leaving, and with whom am I leaving it.

As a wise pastor evangelist once said: *I never saw a U-haul truck following a hearse.*

Or as Socrates once quipped so aptly: "If I had one thing to proclaim aloud for all to hear, it would be this – I would climb to the tallest mountain in all of Greece and announce: *People of Greece, why do you spend so much time, pay so much attention, and toil so laboriously, to turn every rock and pebble to discover gold, silver and precious stones, and pay so little attention, time and toil on those to whom one day you must leave it all?"*

Index

49494708R00193

Made in the USA
Charleston, SC
25 November 2015